The Tower Hamlets Rifle Volunteer Brigade
(1st Tower Hamlets Rifle Volunteers)

THE
TOWER HAMLETS RIFLE VOLUNTEER BRIGADE

(1st TOWER HAMLETS RIFLE VOLUNTEERS).

A SHORT HISTORY

COMPILED FROM

Official Documents and other Sources,

BY

Col. E. T. RODNEY WILDE, V.D.,

LIEUT.-COL. COMMANDANT, 1890-1902.

SECOND EDITION.

Enlarged and Revised to date and change of Designation.

LONDON:
PRINTED AND PUBLISHED BY CONINGHAM BROS., LIMEHOUSE, E.

1903.

Entered at Stationers' Hall.

THE TOWER HAMLETS RIFLE VOLUNTEER BRIGADE.

THE TOWER HAMLETS was represented as a military body as far back as 1643, when the Tower Hamlets Regiment of Trained Bands took part in a Muster held in the New Artillery Gardens and adjacent fields on Tuesday, 26th September of that year, during the absence from London of certain other of the Trained Bands at the Parliamentary Wars, where they appear to have served with considerable distinction under the Earl of Essex.

The place of rendezvous and order of march for the several regiments were laid down ; the Tower Hamlets having to assemble in Smithfield and Aldersgate Street, and to march next after the City Regiments ; the Auxiliaries of the Hamlets were to assemble in Fenchurch and Gracechurch Streets to march in rear of the Southwark Regiment.

The Tower Hamlets Regiment on the day of the muster consisted of 849 Muskets, 385 Pikes, and 70 Officers, making a total of 1304, with 7 Ensigns or Colours. The colour was a red flag, with the motto, "Jehovah Providebit," within two palms forming a wreath, and small sprays of palm in each corner, all in silver. The Commanding Officer was the Lieutenant of the Tower, and the Regiment was recruited within the limits of the "Hamlets" belonging to the Tower.

On the 16th October, 1643, the Yellow Regiment of Auxiliaries of the Tower Hamlets was called out with others and served under Sir William Waller, taking part in the skirmish at Alton, Farnham, and Basing House, returning to London on Wednesday, the 20th December.

The Court of Common Council called the Tower Hamlets Auxiliaries out on 30th September, 1644. No doubt the Hamlets Regiments were present at other musters of the Trained Bands.

We find in the history of the Honourable Artillery Company frequent mention of the Tower Hamlets; in October, 1675, the Minutes of the Artillery Company record—

> Directions were given that no Drumbeaters were to be permitted to beat to the Company except those belonging to the Trained Bands of the Tower Hamlets.

On the 27th November, 1753, the Tower Hamlets Regiment attended on Tower Hill, lining the way to the steps of the booth, where the Lord Mayor, Sir Thomas Rawlinson, was sworn in on succeeding Sir E. Ironside, deceased; on 9th November, 1761, when Lord Mayor Sir Samuel Fludyer entertained George the Third and his Queen at the Guildhall, the Trained Bands of the Tower Hamlets joined the Artillery Company to keep the roads clear for the procession through the City.

The London Trained Bands were re-organized as Volunteers in 1794.

In February, 1795, the Tower Hamlets Volunteers applied for permission to use the Artillery Ground at Finsbury twice a week, but were informed that their request could not be complied with. About a hundred years later a similar request was again refused.

When the Volunteers were required to meet the threatened invasion by Napoleon in 1798, corps were formed in the Tower Hamlets.

At the Reviews of the Volunteer and Associated Corps held in Hyde Park on the 4th June, 1799, and on same date in 1800, the following Tower Hamlets Regiments were present:—

District.	4th June, 1799. Commander.	Numbers.	4th June, 1800. Commander.	Numbers.
Mile End	—	—	Capt. Liptrap	90
Whitechapel	Capt. Rhodes	95	Capt. Rhodes	102
Ratcliff	Capt. Browne	67	Capt. Boulcott	65
Limehouse	Capt. Richardson	46	Capt. Richardson	51
Blackwall and Poplar	Capt. Perry	73	Capt. Perry	68
Bromley	—	—	Capt. Stonard	49
Shoreditch	Capt. Marshall	60	Capt. Marshall	58
Hackney	Capt. Williams	87	Capt. Williams	94
Wapping	Capt. James	43	—	—
Christchurch	—	—	Capt. Toulmin	50

The Tower Hamlets were present at the Review of Volunteers held in Hyde Park by King George the Third on 26th October, 1803, and also on 18th June, 1814, at the Review held in Hyde Park on the occasion of the visit of the Allied Sovereigns the last public appearance of the Volunteer Force of that period

Present 18th June, 1814:—

Tower Hamlets	350
Whitechapel	445
Mile End	330
S. George's East	230
Ratcliff	183
Shoreditch	294
Bromley	175
Bethnal Green	166
Christchurch	180

The Volunteer Corps in the Tower Hamlets in 1803 are shewn by a Return presented to the House of Commons of the Volunteer and Yeomanry Corps of the United Kingdom, whose services had been accepted by His Majesty in pursuance of the following Order :—

Wednesday, 10th day of August, 1803.

Resolved, Unanimously.—That the thanks of the House be given to the several Volunteer and Yeomanry Corps of the United Kingdom for the Promptitude and Zeal with which, at a crisis, the most momentous to their Country, they have associated for its Defence.

Ordered, Unanimously.—That a Return be prepared, to be laid before this House, in the next Session of Parliament, of all Volunteer and Yeomanry Corps, whose services shall have been then accepted by His Majesty, describing each Corps; in order that such Return may be entered on the Journals of this House, and the Patriotic Example of such Voluntary Exertions transmitted to Posterity.

Volunteers.	Commandant.	Infantry: Number of Companies.	Infantry: Establishment per Company.	Infantry: Total.	Field Officers.	Captains.	Subalterns.	Staff Officers.	Sergeants.	Corporals.	Drummers.	Effective Rank & File.	Date of Acceptance.	Terms of Service.
Mile End	Lieut.-Col. Liptrap	6	50	300	2	6	12	2	16	12	13	300	15 Aug, 1808	According to Defence Acts.
Whitechapel	Lieut.-Col. Craven	7	73	511	2	7	15	4	23	28	14	511	,, Do.	,,
1st Regt. Tower Hamlets	Lieut.-Col. Mellish	8	68	544	2	8	16	2	25	24	16	450	,, Do.	,,
St. George, Middlesex	Major Splidt	5	60	300	1	5	10	3	15	15	10	215	,, Do.	,,
Ratcliff	Major Boulcott	3	60	180	1	3	6	3	10	6	10	174	,, Do.	,,
St. Ann, Limehouse	Major Richardson	4	60	240	1	4	8	3	13	12	10	240	,, Do.	,,
Blackwall and Poplar	Major Wells	4	68	272	1	3	8	2	12	12	4	272	17 Do.	,,
Bromley, St. Leonard	Major Stonard	3	60	180	1	4	8	2	7	6	8	160	,, Do.	,,
Shoreditch	Major Marshall	4	72	288	1	8	16	4	11	11	8	287	,, Do.	,,
Royal West India Dock Regt.	Lieut.-Col. Hebbert	8	63	504	3	8	6	0	26	26	10	500	19 Do.	,,
Hackney	Major Powell	3	72	216	1	4	6	2	9	9	8	180	13 Sep.	,,
Christchurch, Middlesex	Major Stephens	4	60	240	1	3	8	2	12	12	6	180	,, Do.	,,
Bethnal Green	Major Carrick	3	66	198	1	4	6	3	9	9	6	189	,, Do.	,,
Loyal Bow	Captain Hickes	2	75	150	0	3	4	0	7	5	6	102	,, Do.	,,
Hackney Riflemen	Captain Williams	1	50	50	0	1	2	0	3	0	0	32	,, Do.	,,
		65		4173	18	65	131	31	198	187	129	3742		

There were no Cavalry or Artillery.

The allowances required and granted for pay and clothing were:—Ratcliff, Shoreditch, Hackney, and Hackney Riflemen, none; Whitechapel, 20/- per man, no clothing; and Royal West India Dock Regiment, for Adjutant, 20/- a man, no clothing; and all the others received the "August allowances."

Captain Williams, mentioned as commanding the Hackney Riflemen, was present at a meeting of Commanding Officers, called by the Duke of York on 17th April, 1798, in consequence of the fear of an invasion. The names of several of the Commanders at the Reviews of 1799 and 1800 appear in the Return.

The uniforms were scarlet with blue facings, the breeches or pantaloons being blue or white; the Officers wore gold lace.

It may be of interest to give the pay and allowances of that date (1804).

"Memorandum for the information of Paymasters and others, of the Pay and Allowances that will be granted to Officers, Non-Com. Officers, Drummers or Fifers, and Private Men of Corps of Volunteer Infantry, when assembled under competent authority, on any invasion or appearance of the enemy in force on the coast, or for the suppression of Rebellion or Insurrection; or when voluntarily assembled with the approbation of His Majesty, signified through one of His Principal Secretaries of State, for the purpose of improving themselves in Military Exercise."

IN SOUTH BRITAIN.

Pay as usually borne on the Establishment.

COMMISSIONED AND WARRANT OFFICERS.

	Per Diem.
Colonel	£1 2 6
(The Colonel or Commandant receives also as pay the sum of Sixpence per diem for each Company in lieu of warrant men)	
Lieut.-Colonel Commandant, or Lieut.-Colonel	0 15 11
Major Commandment or Major	0 14 1
Captain Commandant or Captain	0 9 5
Lieutenant	0 4 8
Second Lieutenant or Ensign	0 3 8
Adjutant (and allowance for maintenace of 1 horse)	0 8 0
Surgeon	0 9 5
Assistant Surgeon	0 7 6
Quarter Master	0 4 8
Chaplain or Officiating Clergyman, for each Sunday he shall officiate	0 10 0

When the Adjutant, Surgeon, or Assistant Surgeon hold other Commissions in the Corps, their pay as Staff Officers is as follows :—Adjutant, 4s.; Surgeon, 4s.; Assistant Surgeon, 3s. per diem. In case the Surgeon keeps a horse for the performance of his Regimental duty, his pay is made up to 11s. 4d. per diem.

NON-COMMISSIONED OFFICERS, DRUMMERS OR FIFERS, AND PRIVATE MEN :

	Per Diem.
Sergeant-Major	0 2 0¾
Quarter-Master-Sergeant	0 2 0¾
Sergeant	0 1 6¾
Corporal	0 1 2¼
Drummer or Fifer	0 1 1¾
Private Man	0 1 0

ALLOWANCE TO COMMISSIONED OFFICERS :

To Captains of Companies.

Allowance in lieu of Non-effectives, and for the repair of arms and other contingent expenses.

	Per Diem.
For a Company not exceeding 50 Private Men as established	0 2 1
More than 50 and less than 76	0 2 7
76 and upwards	0 3 1

There was also an allowance of One Penny per diem for Beer Money. A sum in proportion to the length of time for which it was agreed to assemble, but not exceeding One Guinea, was to be advanced towards providing necessaries. Regimental allowances were made for Postage, Stationery, Stores, &c., and for Carriage of Baggage.

Any Volunteer attending the exercise of his Corps for the proper number of days was exempt from Ballot for the Militia.

The attendance required was 8 days at least in the course of the 4 months next preceding each return, unless absent with leave or from sickness.

Any Volunteer attending for 24 days in any period of 4 successive months, or within any two successive periods of 4 months each, was entitled to exemption, and was returned as an effective member.

The returns were made on 1st April, August and December in each year.

The T.H.R.V.B. possesses interesting relics of the 1st Regiment Tower Hamlets Volunteers of that date : namely, two plates, which were probably the ornaments of an Officer's and a Private's cross-belt ; they measure 3¼ in. by 2¼ in. and 2⅞ in. by 2 in. respectively.

They are both Silver, Hall-marked, Birmingham, 1803.

These were exhibited in the Military Exhibition at Chelsea in 1890.

There are also a pair of silk Colours of a large size. We here give a print of one, which measures 6 ft. 6 in. by 5 ft. 2 in., and it bears the date of 1798.

The Colours were shown at the Military Exhibition at Chelsea in 1890.

The Regiment has been presented with a very interesting document—the original roll of the Ratcliff Division of the Tower Hamlets Volunteers.

It is a vellum sheet, 33 in. long by 27 in. wide, and is headed—

RATCLIFF VOLUNTEERS.

AT A GENERAL MEETING, SEPTEMBER 5TH, 1803,

G. HARPER, D.D., in the Chair.

Declaration.

WE, the undersigned Members of the Ratcliff Division of the Tower Hamlets Volunteers (having taken the Oath of Allegiance) Do hereby Declare our Attachment to our beloved King and invaluable Constitution, and that we have Associated to learn the Use of Arms for the purpose of protecting and Defending the same . . . . That we will serve without Pay, and hold ourselves in readiness at all times to Assist the Civil Power . . . . . That in case of Actual Invasion we will march to any part of the Kingdom as may be required by [His Majesty . . . . That we hold ourselves bound to conform to the most punctual Attendance, regular Conduct, and strict Decepline *(sic)* . . . .

Then the signatures follow in five columns, filling up the front, and being continued on the back, the Reverend Chairman heading the list. The front contains 234 names, and there are 151 on the other side. There are very few instances of crosses instead of signatures, so that the Volunteers were probably of the Professional, Merchant or Trader classes.

All those who signed on the front, and in the first column on the other side, appear to have been enrolled at the date of the Meeting. Further on in the roll other dates are entered, the last being October 20th, 1813, after which only one signature is written.

The Roll included those then serving as Volunteers in the Ratcliff Corps which was present at the Reviews of 4th June, 1799 and 1800.

Major Boulcott, who is given in the Return made to the House of Commons as Commandant of the Ratcliff Corps, signed fourth. He was in command of the Corps at the Review of 1800.

There is also in the Officers' Ante-room at Headquarters a large side-drum which belonged to the 2nd Grenadier Battalion of the East India London Volunteers, and was first used at the presentation of Colours at Lord's Cricket Ground 27th July, 1797.

The drum has inscribed on it :—
"ROYAL EAST INDIA VOLUNTEERS.
AUSPICIO REGIS ET SENATUS ANGLIÆ."

The title is in a circle round a coat of arms, with a lion on each side bearing a flag as supporters, the motto in a scroll beneath the arms.

There is also a coloured representation of a Private of the Ratcliff Volunteers in the position of "Make Ready" (front Rank), with instructions underneath :—
"At the word 'ready' the firelock is brought to the same position as recover, at the same time cocking it."

The print is marked, "London, Pub. Sep. 21, 1798, at Ackermanns, 101 Strand."

Although in 1803 there were 464,000 effective Volunteers, the force gradually diminished when the immediate danger ceased, and before the war closed with the abdication of Napoleon in 1814, it was replaced by a new force called "Local Militia." The Volunteer Corps having been relieved from further duty, their arms were called in, by an order issued from the Horse Guards in June, 1814.

THE TOWER HAMLETS RIFLE VOLUNTEER BRIGADE.

The T.H.R.V.B. has been formed out of three of the twelve original Rifle Corps of the Tower Hamlets, which was 89th in order of precedence of Counties, as the circular issued from the War Office on 12th May, 1859, sanctioning the formation of Rifle Volunteer Corps under the Volunteer Act of 1804, was not taken advantage of in the district till twelve months afterwards.

PARTICULARS OF THE ORIGINAL TOWER HAMLETS RIFLE VOLUNTEER CORPS.

Original No.	Head-quarters.	Date Raised.	Remarks.	Enrolled Strength. 1862.	1872.
1	Dalston	1860	Disbanded, 1860	—	—
2	Hackney	,,	Joined the 4th in 1868, and became the T.H.R.V.B.	648	833
3	Whitechapel	,,	Now with 7th and 10th, forms the present 2nd T.H.R.V.	237	225
4	Shoreditch	,,	Joined 2nd in 1868, and became the T.H.R.V.B.	296	—
5	Kingsland	,,	Disbanded, 1862	—	—
6	Hoxton	,,	Joined T.H.R.V.B. in 1874	577	731
7	Mile End	,,	Joined 3rd in 1880	153	348
8	West India Docks	,,	Joined 26th Middlesex in 1868	100	—
9	London Docks	,,	Joined do. in 1864	99	—
10	Mile End	,,	Joined 3rd in 1880	132	236
11	Goodman's Fields	1861	Disbanded in 1864	120	—
12	Stoke Newington	,,	Joined L.R.B. 1870	128	—

It may perhaps be interesting to give such accounts of the three Corps—2nd, 4th, and 6th—out of which the T.H.R.V.B. was formed, as we can gather from records, regimental orders, and other information available.

THE SECOND TOWER HAMLETS RIFLE VOLUNTEER CORPS.

This Corps was formed early in 1860, with seven Companies, as follows :—

    No. 1, at Hackney, under Captain Gwillim
    No. 2 ,, Dalston ,, Captain Laws
    No. 3 ,, Bow ,, Captain Byas
    No. 4 ,, Poplar ,, Captain Samuda
    No. 5 ,, and ,, Captain Holt
    No. 6 ,, Limehouse ,, Captain Wigram
    No. 7 ,, Clapton ,, Captain Gibbs

with Headquarters first at Arnold House, Richmond Road, Dalston, afterwards removed to Pembroke Hall, Lamb Lane, South Hackney, Colonel Walker being in command till 1867. Captain Armar Lowry, late Captain 30th Foot, was appointed Adjutant, May, 1860, and Sergeant Travis (from the Tower Hamlets Militia), Sergeant Major.

The uniform was Elcho grey with braiding of scarlet and blue (the Tower Hamlets colours) ; head-dress, a demi shako with " cheese-cutter " peak, a red and blue pompon, brown belts.

Before Bands were allowed, about twenty Members of No. 1, 2 and 3 Companies met once a week to practice various instruments, and marched at the head of the Corps on several occasions until Regimental Bands were authorised.

Colonel Holt and Colonel Wigram, two of the subsequent Commandants of the T.H.R.V.B., received their first Commissions in this Corps as Captains in April, 1860.

The Corps took part in most of the gatherings of the London Volunteers, and for several years held a very successful Regimental Camp at Ilford.

The Corps was present at the Review held by the Queen in Hyde Park, in 1860.

In 1868 a fusion was effected with the Fourth Corps, the then vacant number of first taken, and the title of "The Tower Hamlets Rifle Volunteer Brigade" assumed ; there were 16 Companies, the services of both the Adjutants—Captain Lowry of the 2nd, and Captain Schreiber of the 4th, being retained for a time. Captain Schreiber however was transferred to the 1st Administrative Battalion, Cambridgeshire, in July, 1873.

The 8th and 9th Corps were attached to the 2nd Corps, until they joined the 26th Middlesex.

THE FOURTH TOWER HAMLETS RIFLE VOLUNTEER CORPS.

This Corps was raised in St. Leonards, Shoreditch, in 1860. It consisted of Five Companies, was commanded by Major W. F. de la Rue, and was attached to the Sixth Corps for Administrative purposes, using the same Headquarters, and parading with the Sixth for Battalion Drills, Field Days, Inspection, &c. ; separate Regimental Orders were however issued from time to time, as to Corps matters, Company Drills, &c. There was an annual subscription of One Guinea, payable quarterly in advance.

The uniform was grey with red braiding, demi shako with a "cheese-cutter" peak, and a plume, changed in 1862 to a red pompon, and black belts.

On Wednesday, 3rd July, 1861, a Stand of Colours was presented to the Corps, in the grounds of the Ironmongers' Alms Houses, Hackney Road, the Sixth furnishing a Guard of Honour.

With the Sixth it took part in the Easter Monday Review at Brighton, in 1862, and a Field Day on Whit Monday in same year, held at Earl Cowper's Park, Panshanger, under Lord Ranelagh.

On the 26th July, 1862, the Chaplain showed the interest he took in the Corps by entertaining the Members at a cold collation in the School-room of St. James the Less, Victoria Park. No. 5 Company was allowed to use these schools for Company Drill.

Towards the close of 1864 the Corps was raised to a consolidated Battalion. Captain Schreiber, late Lieutenant of 1st Foot, being appointed Adjutant in December. Colour-Sergeant J. Woodham, from the 59th Regiment, was appointed

Sergeant-Major in 1862, and continued in that rank until his retirement in August, 1882.

Colonel James Thomson, who had been Major in the Sixth, was gazetted Lieutenant-Colonel in April, 1865.

In 1868 it joined the Second Corps, Colonel Thomson commanding the united Corps until his death in 1870.

THE SIXTH TOWER HAMLETS RIFLE VOLUNTEER CORPS.

(THE NORTH=EAST LONDON RIFLES.)

The N.E.L.R. (the 6th Tower Hamlets), was formed in Hoxton in 1860, with an establishment of eight Companies. The title of North-East London was borne by a Volunteer Regiment sixty years before, which, under command of Colonel Sir R. C. Glyn, was present nearly 300 strong at the Reviews held by King George the Third in Hyde Park on 4th June, 1799, and 1800.

Colonel George Henry Money was the Commanding Officer until his resignation on 25th June, 1873, when Colonel J. H. Mapleson succeeded to the command, which he retained until the amalgamation in January, 1874.

Captain C. N. Walmisley (late Captain the King's Own Militia) was appointed Adjutant in November, 1860 ; he was succeeded in December, 1872, by Captain B. H. Burge, half-pay, late 59th foot. Sergeant W. H. Tustin, late of the 50th was appointed Sergeant-Major in July, 1860, and retired in March, 1877.

The uniform was grey, with red and blue braidings, a demi shako with "cheese-cutter" peak, white plume, changed for a blue and white tuft in 1862 ; a full sized shako was subsequently adopted, with the old shaped peak, and blue and white tuft ; the belts and accoutrements, originally brown were altered to black in October, 1863. In undress, the Officers wore black frock coats very similar to the Guards, black trousers with an oak leaf pattern braid stripe, and cap with peak.

The Headquarters were at first in Rosemary Street, Southgate Road, but in August, 1861, the premises in Shaftesbury

Street, formerly known as the "Albert Saloon," were taken and converted into the very good Headquarters, Drill Hall, etc., which the T.H.R.V.B. still occupies, with Parade Ground adjoining.

It may be of interest to note that the Honourable Artillery Company had their shooting marks and butts across the Finsbury Fields, passing Rosemary Branch, and on to Islington Green ; the marks began about where the "Eagle" now stands, so most probably the Company shot over the site of these Headquarters and Ground.

A subscription of £1 a year was payable by all members quarterly, in advance, till about 1864 ; until 1865 the travelling expenses to Reviews, Field Days, etc., were paid by each member. Members, too, paid part of the cost of the uniform, £2, in 1864, reduced to £1 10s. in the next year, and in 1871 to £1, and then gradually done away with. Great coats were issued for a payment of 9s.

The Officers paid an annual subscription according to a scale laid down in the rules.

In the Battalion Orders of 31st January, 1865, it is notified that the Secretary of State approved of the Regiment being officially designated "North-East London Rifles."

The Battalion having gradually increased to ten Companies, authority for an eleventh was given in February, 1866, and in March following a twelfth was authorised.

The Corps possessed a handsome pair of Colours which appeared at Church Parades and on other occasions (and which the writer has carried), until an order was issued forbidding the use of Colours to Volunteer Corps.

A large handsome Silver Challenge Vase was presented in 1864, and became the chief Regimental Challenge Cup.

In 1867 the Proprietors of the "Philharmonic," Islington, gave a handsome Silver Cup for competition amongst the Corps in the neighbourhood. The North East London winning it that year and again in 1868, it became the property of the Corps and was made a Regimental Challenge Cup.

In 1867 in consequence of "Fenian" alarms, guards were kept at Headquarters day and night until the arms were removed to the Tower.

On 14th November, 1867, a meeting was held to consider the question of changing the uniform to scarlet, which it was decided not to do.

In January, 1868, a Club was formed at Headquarters for Members of the Corps; it had a successful career for some years. There was a gymnasium and school of arms carried on in the Hall.

There was for a short time a Cadet Corps with a Band of its own; it attended the Review of Cadets at the Crystal Palace on 11th September, 1861, under command of Ensign Wilde.

Church Parades were very frequent at first, but presently became annual and were generally held at St. Paul's Cathedral.

Battalion Drills were on Saturdays in uniform at the Tower, in the Grounds of the Charterhouse, and Victoria Park, where blank firing was then allowed, and at other convenient places.

The Ranges at Plumstead, Child's Hill, and later on at High Beech, Loughton, and Tottenham were used for target practice.

It may be interesting to give the Scheme of the movements arranged to be executed at the Annual Inspection in 1863:—

THE BATTALION WILL ASSEMBLE IN OPEN COLUMN OF COMPANIES—RIGHT IN FRONT.

The Inspection will proceed as follows:—

Tell off the Battalion, p. 226 of "Field Exercise, 1862," Shilling Edition.
Left wheel into line, p. 227. Fix bayonets.
Rear Rank take open order, p. 232. March, Stand at ease.
On the General coming—Attention—Shoulder arms—General salute—Present arms—Shoulder arms. (The General will ride down the line from right, and return along the rear.)
Rear Rank take close order—March; p. 236.
Open Column, right in front; p. 277.
March past in quick time, pp. 86 and 90.
The Column will close on No. 1, p. 249.
March past in close Column.
Column will open out to wheeling distance from the rear, p. 252.

As Companies in line. Rear ranks take open order — March. No. 1 stand fast. Remaining Companies—Stand at ease.

(The General will examine arms, &c., Captains calling their men to attention, fixing bayonets, and bringing arms to the port just before the General comes up, then saluting and going round with him ; and when he has passed, unfixing bayonets, closing ranks, and standing at ease.)

Parade—Attention.

Left wheel into line, p. 227.

(Manual and Platoon by the Senior Major.)

Line will advance, p. 229.

Battalion will dress by the right, p. 238.

Retire by Companies from the right in rear of the left, p. 287.

Change direction to the left, p. 256 (the space being contracted.)

Front turn. Form line to the reverse flank, p. 303.

Quarter distance Column right in front, facing to the rear on No. 5, pp. 297 and 298.

Take ground to the right in fours, p. 273.

Deploy on No. 4, p. 323. (Pp. 315 to 322.)

Right Company to the front ; remaining Companies on the move ; right wheel, p. 281.

Change direction to the left, p. 256 (the space being contracted).

By Companies—Left wheel into line. Forward, by your centre.

By Companies—Left wheel. Forward, by your right.

On the march close to quarter distance on present leading Company. Remaining Companies Double—Halt, p. 251.

Column will countermarch by files, p. 268.

Column will advance.

Change front to rear by wheel of subdivisions round centre on the march, p. 264.

Column will wheel to its left, pp. 261 and 263 (when square—Forward).

Column will retire (right about turn). Halt—Front.

Deploy on the leading Company, p. 315.

Line will advance, p. 229.

From left of Companies pass by fours to the rear, pp. 245 and 246.

Front turn—Right wheel into line—Forward.

From right of Companies, pass by fours to the rear, p. 245.

Front turn.

On leading Company Form Square, p. 333. Prepare for Cavalry, &c., p. 338.

Square will retire, p. 340. Halt—Reform Column, p. 338.

Column will retire—Front turn—Double.

On leading Company Form Square, p. 336. (Colonel says " sections outwards.")

Re-form Column.

Column will retire ; Column will wheel to its left, p. 268 (rear rank in front). Halt—Front.

Deploy on No. 3, p. 323.
Battalion will advance in direct echelon of Companies at five paces distance from the right, p. 366.
Echelon will wheel to its right. By Companies right wheel, p. 370.
Echelon will wheel to its left. By Companies left wheel, p. 370.
Form Company Squares, p. 339. Re-form echelon.
Echelon will retire.
Form line on the present leading Company, p. 369.
Line will advance.
Retire by Companies from both flanks in rear of the centre, p. 291.
Front turn. Form line on the two leading Companies, p. 308.
  (Remaining Companies outwards wheel—Forward.)
Quarter Distance Column right in front on No. 6, p. 297.
Column will advance.
Column will wheel to left, p. 261.
Deploy on the leading Company, p. 315.
Change front to the right on No. 8; right thrown back the quarter circle, p. 359.
  (Remaining Companies—Right about face. On the move; right wheel; quick march; forward.)
Fix bayonets; Shoulder arms; Rear rank take open order; march.
Line will advance in review order, p. 506; by your centre; slow march; halt. GENERAL SALUTE.

We have the Scheme for the Annual Inspection, 5th August, 1865, when certain movements were similarly laid down.

In 1865 a prize was offered to the best drilled Company, the award to be made on the performance of certain movements. Challenge Medals were given, to be retained if won three years, gold for Colour-Sergeant, silver for Sergeants, and bronze for Rank and File.

The following was issued to the Umpires.

TEST PAPER OF COMPANIES OF
NORTH-EAST LONDON RIFLES
AT A COMPETITIVE EXAMINATION IN DRILL
AT HEADQUARTERS, SATURDAY, 29TH JULY, 1865.

THE HIGHEST NUMBER OF MARKS IS SEVEN.

1. Assemble on Coverer, Column right in front.
2. As a Company in line.
3. By Sub-Divisions on the Left, Backward wheel.
4. Left wheel into line.
5. Line will retire.
6. Right Section to the front, remaining Sections on the move, Right wheel.

7. Change direction to the left.
8. Right form Company.
9. Form fours left.
10. Left wheel.
11. Left about Form Company.
12. (File Marching) Right face, Quick march—Halt.
13. Front form Company.
14. Right close—Quick march.
15. (As in Column right in front) Counter-march by Files.
16. Diagonal March.
17. Form Subdivisions.
18. Form Company.
19. Manual. Rear rank take open order; Secure and present.
20. Platoon. In quick time—Load—Volley and Shoulder.
21. Form Company Square.
22. Re-form Company.
23. Open Column right in front.
24. Left wheel into line.
25. Non-Commissioned Officers.

In 1866 and 1867 a similar Competition was again held. The prize was won in these three years by No. 5 Company, Commanded by Colour-Sergeant Towner, and therefore became entitled to retain the Challenge Medals.

The Battalion frequently joined neighbouring Corps, Artillery, Engineers and Infantry for Field Days, Drill and Route Marches. It took part in Field Days on Whit Monday, 1861, in Regent's Park, next year in Earl Cowper's Park at Panshanger, and in 1867 at Windsor. On 18th October, 1862, the Corps proceeded to Harwich to take part in a Field Day which, however, was put a stop to by the weather. On Boxing Day, 1861, the N.E.L.R. had a Route March to Chingford and back; in the next year we find it at Caterham; on the 20th June, 1863, there were operations at Wanstead, of which we are able to give the Programme in the form in which it was issued:

PROGRAMME OF THE BRIGADE FIELD DAY AT
WANSTEAD, SATURDAY, JUNE 20TH, 1863,
UNDER VISCOUNT RANELAGH.

An invading force is supposed to have come up the Thames and landed at Barking, and one of his reconnoitering parties (represented by the South Middlesex) has fallen in with a Brigade of

Volunteers—consisting of the Custom House Battalions and the three Tower Hamlets Battalions, under Lieutenant-Colonel Buxton, M.P.,—which have been posted where several roads meet at Leytonstone, to observe the enemy. The reconnoitering party is attacked, and compelled to take refuge in the large empty house near Wigram's Lane, from every window of which they keep up a heavy fire upon the 1st Tower Hamlets which surrounds them, supported by the 2nd Tower Hamlets; Lieutenant-Colonel Buxton, meanwhile, protecting his left flank (which lies towards the invading army) by throwing forward the Custom House Battalions and the 4th and 6th Tower Hamlets into the Wanstead Avenues.

The enemy hearing the firing, sends forward a Brigade—represented by Colonel Whitehead's, Colonel Capper's, and Colonel Davis's Battalions, under Lord Ranelagh—to the rescue of the reconnoitering party. Lord Ranelagh drives back Colonel Buxton's pickets and skirmishers, upon which the latter brings up the 2nd Tower Hamlets, and, both sides deploying into line, a brisk skirmish ensues. Lord Ranelagh pushes forward his right, in order to cut Colonel Buxton off from the Leytonstone Road to London, and also in order to force a communication with the reconnoitering party in the house. Colonel Buxton, at length, finding himself overpowered by Lord Ranelagh, retires in direct echelon of Battalions from the left; his left Battalion retiring by fours from the right of Companies, through the rough ground near the edge of the forest; his centre Battalion in double column of sub-divisions down the main avenue; his right Battalion, in open column of Companies, from the left in rear of the right, along a forest road. Withdrawing the 1st Tower Hamlets from the attack on the house, Colonel Buxton changes front to the left, with a view of retreating across the flats to reach the Stratford Road to London, and deploys and retires by wings. Lord Ranelagh also changes front to the left, and deploys, and endeavours to outflank Colonel Buxton's right; but this manœuvre is prevented by a vigorous charge with the bayonet, before which Lord Ranelagh's Brigade takes to flight, but is speedily rallied. Meanwhile, however, Colonel Buxton's Brigade has effected its retreat, and the skirmish comes to an end.

Lord Ranelagh will then put the two Brigades through a series of movements, with which the affair will close.

The Corps attended all the Easter Monday Field Days from 1861, and was at the Reviews held at Wimbledon at the close of the meetings of the National Rifle Association.

The North-East London Rifles was in Hyde Park on the entry of the Princess of Wales into London, on the 7th March, 1863; and the Review there on 28th May, 1864, to celebrate the Queen's Birthday; also took part in the March Past before the Duke of Cambridge on 23rd June, 1866; and the Review at Wimbledon, in honour of the Sultan of Turkey, on 20th July, 1867, which closed the N.R.A. meeting of that year. It was also at the Review by the Queen at Windsor, on 20th June, 1868, and was present at all the gatherings of Metropolitan Regiments.

The North-East London Rifles had for several years a Regimental Camp at Wimbledon during the National Rifle Association meetings.

From time to time Guards of Honour were furnished at various places in the district.

The prizes were distributed each year, generally at the Headquarters, the Lord Mayor and Lady Mayoress of the year, General McMurdo, Lord Ranelagh, and other persons of note presiding on several occasions.

In 1865 Colonel Richardson-Gardner became Hon. Colonel in place of Sir Henry de Hoghton, Bart., who joined the Fourth Corps.

Medals—with a red ribbon—were given in 1866 to those Members who had been efficient for five consecutive years Twelve Officers and 71 men were recipients at the Prize Night on 6th December, 1866; a bar was afterwards added for each subsequent two years—the medals were not however allowed to be worn.

In 1871 the Corps was armed with Sniders in place of the old Enfield Rifles.

Companies were lettered instead of being numbered in 1873.

The coming incorporation with the Tower Hamlets Rifle Volunteer Brigade was shown in 1873 by a united Field Day at Hendon, on 23rd August; a Church Parade at St. Paul's, on 31st August; and a March Out and Battalion Drill on 11th October.

Colonel Wilde was Gazetted Ensign to the N.E.L.R., in June, 1861, and Colonel Fletcher, Lieutenant, in June, 1867.

THE TOWER HAMLETS RIFLE VOLUNTEER BRIGADE.

The Regiment may be considered to have become complete in January, 1874. when the following Regimental Orders were issued :—

TOWER HAMLETS RIFLE VOLUNTEER BRIGADE

(NORTH-EAST LONDON RIFLES INCORPORATED).

Regimental Orders for the Week ending 17th January, 1874.

The authority for incorporating the 6TH TOWER HAMLETS (North-East London Rifles) with the 1ST TOWER HAMLETS having been received from the War Office, the amalgamation takes effect as from 1st January, 1874.

The united Corps will bear the name of the 1ST TOWER HAMLETS RIFLE VOLUNTEER CORPS, OR TOWER HAMLETS RIFLE VOLUNTEER BRIGADE, and will consist of 16 Companies, with two Lieutenant-Colonels and the usual number of Officers.

The Headquarters of the Brigade will be on and from this day at 112, Shaftesbury Street, Hoxton.

The use of the premises, No. 21, White Lion Street, is discontinued from this date.

The following statement shows the re-arrangement of the several Companies, the Corps to which each formerly belonged, and the names of the Officers at present commanding them, viz. :—

A.	(Late T.H.B.)	Captain Taylor.
B.	(Late A. & L., N.E.L)	Lieutenant Clark.
C.	(Late B., T.H.B.)	Captain Hunter.
D.	(Late B., N.E.L.)	Captain Tipper.
E.	(Late C. & D., T.H.B.)	Captain De la Mare.
F.	(Late C. & H., N.E.L.)	Captain Wilde.
G.	(Late E., T.H.B.)	Captain Gole.
H.	(Late D., N.E.L.)	Captain De Metz.
J.	(Late F. I. & K., T.H.B.)	Captain Ronaldson.
K.	(Late E., N.E.L.)	Lieutenant Burt.
L.	(Late G., T.H.B.)	Captain Purser.
M.	(Late F. & G., N.E.L.)	Captain Silk.
N.	(Late H. & J., T.H.B.)	Captain Bull.
O.	(Late J., N.E.L.)	Captain Fletcher.
P.	(Late O., T.H.B.)	Captain Hill.
Q.	(Late K., N.E.L.)	Captain Oppenheim.

Full particulars relating to the several Companies will be posted in the Drill Hall.

Saturday (this day), MARCH OUT AND BATTALION DRILL. Muster at Shaftesbury Street, at 6.30, for parade at 7 o'clock precisely. Shakos and leggings to be worn. Bands to attend.

In consequence of the many arrangements to be made, and the new books required by reason of the amalgamation, there will be no drill next week.

BY ORDER.
(Signed) B. H. BURGE, Captain and Adjutant,
Headquarters, Tower Hamlets Rifle Brigade.
112, Shaftesbury St., Hoxton,
January 10th, 1874.

Colonel Holt was Commanding Officer, Colonel Mapleson becoming Junior Lieutenant-Colonel; the other Field Officers being Majors Clifford Wigram, and C. A. Emmett. On the retirement of the latter, Captain Wilde was promoted Major, 21st May, 1879.

Captain Lowry, the Adjutant of the old 2nd Corps, and Captain Burge of the 6th, were Adjutants, Sergeant-Majors Tustin and Woodham continued.

As the 6th did not wear a red stripe on their trousers, an order was issued for this part of their uniform to be sent in to be altered.

In August, 1874, the War Office reduced the Establishment to 12 Companies, and Captain Burge, the Junior Adjutant, was transferred in January, 1876, to the 1st Lanark R.V., Glasgow.

The Companies were, however, not re-arranged till the close of the year, when the four returning the lowest percentage of Efficients on 31st October were transferred to other Companies.

The twelve Companies were formed by the Regimental Orders of 28th November, 1874, as follows :—

A. (late A. & P.) Captain Taylor, Lieutenants Fernyhough and Seaton, Colour-Sergeants Garrett and Sweetman.
B. (late B.) Lieutenant Clark, Colour-Sergeant Voisey.
C. (late O. and Q.) Captain Fletcher, Colour-Sergeants Arnott and Poole.
D. (late E. and C.) Captain De la Mare, Lieutenant Bennett, Colour-Sergeants Costin and Olley.

E. (late J.) Captain Ronaldson, Lieutenant Heiser, Colour-Sergeant Evans.
F. (late J.) Captain Wilde, Lieutenant Thompson, Colour-Sergeant Strugnell.
G. (late G.) Captain Gole, Lieutenant Gole, Colour-Sergeant Arle.
H. (late H.) Captain de Metz, Colour-Sergeant Patmor.
J. (late N.) Captain Bull, Lieutenant Bull, Colour-Sergeants Powley and Griffin.
K. (late K. and D.) Captain Tipper, Lieutenant Burt, Colour-Sergeant Cook.
L. (late L.) Lieutenant Smith, Colour-Sergeant Watson.
M. (late M.) Captain Silk, Colour-Sergeants Towner and Slater.

The regimental badge is the White Tower of the Tower of London :—

The uniform was soon changed to scarlet, for on the 14th November, 1874, it is notified in Orders that the new scarlet uniforms had been approved by the War Office. The frock for Officers' undress was continued, new patterns being adopted from time to time. The Officers' Mess Uniform, when the Battalion was in grey, was a black jacket with rolled collar, red open waistcoat, black trousers, with oak-leaf braid stripe. This was changed to scarlet jacket fastened at the collar, and blue waistcoat. The present rolled collar jacket was adopted in 1897.

As under the localization of the forces then existing, the Brigade was one of the Volunteer Battalions of " Sub-District

No. 49, Middlesex and Metropolitan," the uniform of the line Battalion, the 7th Royal Fusiliers, was adopted—scarlet with blue facings—but as permission could not be obtained for Fusilier busbies, the shako, full size, was continued as the head-dress. In 1878 Helmets were adopted, and in 1880 the black slings of the rifles were changed to white ones.

In July, 1894, the then new pattern Field Service Cap was adopted in place of the Glengarry.

In 1877, the localization scheme underwent revision, and the T.H.R.V.B. became a Volunteer Battalion of The Rifle Brigade. For purposes of drill and discipline, however, it—with other Metropolitan Corps—formed part of a Volunteer Brigade, under the Colonel commanding the Scots Guards, as Brigadier. In 1889 it was transferred to the Grenadier Guards, and formed one of the Battalions of the East London Volunteer Infantry Brigade. In 1902 the Brigades were re-arranged, and the Battalion was posted to the 2nd London Volunteer Infantry Brigade, under the Irish Guards.

On 22nd April, 1876, Quarter-Master Anderson, who had served sixteen years, was buried with military honours.

On the 16th June, 1876, the following announcement appeared in the Battalion Orders :—

> Lieutenant-Colonel Holt, after a service of more than sixteen years, announces that he has tendered his resignation as Commanding Officer. He desires to thank the Staff Officers, Non-Commissioned Officers and Privates for the uniform kindness and support he has received. He congratulates the Regiment upon its good financial position, its many advantages, and the good feeling which pervades all the ranks. He regards with great satisfaction the prospect of continued success, which he hopes will be promoted by the united energy of all, and he has pleasure in stating that Major Clifford Wigram has been recommended for promotion to the rank of Lieutenant-Colonel.

On the 30th June, the following appeared in the *London Gazette* :—

> Lieutenant-Colonel John Holt resigns his commission, and is permitted to retain his rank and wear the uniform of the Corps.
> Major Clifford Wigram to be Lieutenant-Colonel.

Lieutenant-Colonel Mapleson consequently assumed command. Colonel Mapleson also held at the same time a commission in the Honourable Artillery Company as Captain under date of 6th November, 1875.

Colonel Holt continued to take a great interest in the T.H.R.V.B., and was a liberal subscriber to the Prize Fund until his death, in October, 1889.

In 1876, and again in 1877, a Detachment proceeded by Route March to Tring and Dunstable, for the Easter Monday Field Day, starting on the previous Saturday, each man paying his own expenses. At Easter, 1878, a strong Detachment marched to Watford, although there were no operations on the Monday. The T.H.R.V.B. was thus one of the first to form a marching column. Captain, now Colonel, Wilde was in command on each occasion. Later in 1886, 1887 and 1888, Detachments joined the Easter Marching Columns.

In June, 1880, Major Lowry, who had been Adjutant since 1860, retired, and the following appeared in the Battalion Orders of 19th June, 1880 :—

> The following is inserted by leave of the Commanding Officer :—
>
> In taking leave of the Regiment, having served in it as Adjutant for upwards of twenty years, Major Lowry desires to express his sincere thanks for the cordial support and co-operation which he has uninterruptedly received from all ranks.

Captain E. de B. Barnett, 4th King's Own Regiment, was appointed. He, however, being promoted and retiring from the service as Lieutenant-Colonel in October, 1881, Major Schreiber, late 1st Foot, who was for a short time Adjutant of the 4th Corps, was transferred from the 1st Cambridgeshire Rifle Volunteers. In 1882 there was another change of Adjutants; Captain E. R. S. Richardson, of the Prince of Wales's North Staffordshire Regiment, being gazetted in February in place of Major Schreiber. In April, 1884, on appointment to the Royal Military College, Sandhurst, Captain Richardson was succeeded by Captain Maude, of The Rifle

Brigade, and on his term expiring on April 1st, 1889, Captain Money, of the Northumberland Fusiliers, was appointed; he was promoted Major 9th December, 1891, and after his retirement in April, 1894, Lieutenant-Colonel on 23rd November, 1897, and selected to command the 1st Battalion of the Northumberland Fusiliers, serving with them in Egypt in the operations against the Mahdi; he was made C.B.; he was with his Battalion all through the South African Campaign, being promoted Colonel, 29th November, 1900; he was appointed to command of Regimental District No. 24 at Brecon, 21st April, 1902.

The next officer appointed Adjutant was Captain H. A. Coddington, of the Royal Irish Fusiliers, who joined in April, 1894; retiring in April, 1899, he proceeded to take up an appointment as D.A.A.G. in South Africa, received the D.S.O., and, on promotion to Major, 14th September, 1902, was made Brevet Lieutenant-Colonel. Captain D. E. B. Patton-Bethune, of The Rifle Brigade, became Adjutant in April, 1899.

Colonel Mellor having died in June, 1886, in December, Colonel G. H. Moncrieff formerly commanding the Scots Guards, now Lieutenant General, was gazetted Honorary Colonel. He has taken a very active interest in the Regiment and gives annually Prizes to the two best Companies. The conditions are such as to bring out the best work, and the Competition is always very keen.

WINNERS OF GENERAL G. H. MONCRIEFF'S PRIZES.

CONDITIONS.—Strength on 31st October, at end of year; number of efficients; percentage of efficients; percentage present at C.O. Uniform Outdoor Parades; percentage present at Inspection in Uniform if issued; percentage present at Brigade Camp; percentage of recruits enrolled during the volunteer year; total percentages.

1890—One Prize, M Company, Captain V. Dunfee.
1891—One Prize, M Company, Captain V. Dunfee.
1892—1st Prize, E, Brigade Bearer Company.
    2nd Prize, M Company, Captain V. Dunfee.
1893—1st Prize, E, Brigade Bearer Company.
    2nd Prize, J Company, Captain H. Coningham.

1894—1st Prize, E, Brigade Bearer Company.
       2nd Prize, J Company, Captain H. Coningham.
1895—1st Prize, J Company, Captain H. Coningham.
       2nd Prize, E, Brigade Bearer Company.
1896—1st Prize, G Company, Captain E. C. Harris.
       2nd Prize, J Company, Captain J. W. A. Parr.
1897—1st Prize, M Company, Captain V. Dunfee.
1898—1st Prize, M Company, Major V. Dunfee.
       2nd Prize, K Company, Captain E. C. P. Monson.
1899—1st Prize, K Company, Captain E. C. P. Monson.
       2nd Prize, A Company, Captain H. Wells Holland.
1900—1st Prize, K Company, Captain E. C. P. Monson.
       2nd Prize, A Company, Captain H. Wells Holland.
1901—1st Prize, M Company, Captain G. P. Botterill.
       2nd Prize, K Company, Captain E. C. P. Monson.
1902—1st Prize, D Company, Captain W. Stevens.
       2nd Prize, K Company, Captain E. C. P. Monson.

General Moncrieff presents a personal Memento to the Officer in command of the winning Companies.

Colonel Mapleson retired from the Command, and issued the following Battalion Order on 10th November, 1888 :—

> Colonel Mapleson in taking leave of the Tower Hamlets Rifle Brigade, and handing its command over to Colonel Wigram, feels that its interest will be as zealously and heartily felt as it has been by himself for the last nineteen years. Colonel Mapleson, in resigning the command he has prized so highly, begs to tender his special thanks to Colonel Wigram, as well as to all the Officers and men for the constant support and hearty goodwill they have invariably accorded him. Although leaving the Brigade officially, he hopes he will be able from time to time to attend its parades and friendly gatherings, assuring all ranks that its welfare will be his constant wish.

Colonel Mapleson died 14th November, 1901.

Colonel Wigram succeeded to the command on the resignation of Colonel Mapleson, Major Wilde becoming Lieutenant-Colonel, with the honorary rank of Colonel. Colonel Wigram retired in November, 1890, when the following appeared in the Battalion Orders :—

> The following is an extract from the *London Gazette* :—
>
> 1st Tower Hamlets (The Tower Hamlets Rifle Volunteer Brigade).
>
> Lieutenant-Colonel Commandant and Hon. Colonel Clifford Wigram resigns his commission ; also is permitted to retain his

rank, and to continue to wear the uniform of the Corps on his retirement; November 22nd, 1890.

In retiring from the Command of the Tower Hamlets Rifle Brigade, of which Corps he has been a member since the commencement of the Volunteer Force, Colonel Wigram returns his sincere thanks to the Officers, Non-Commissioned Officers (both Staff and Regimental) and members of the Corps for the manner in which they have worked with him for more than 33 years in promoting the efficiency of the regiment. Colonel Wigram begs to assure all the members that, though he can no longer take an active part in promoting the prosperity of the Corps, he will always retain a lively interest in it, and feels confident that all members will strive to maintain it in the high position which it ought to occupy.

Colonel E. T. Rodney Wilde succeeded to the command.

On the resignation of Colonel Clifford Wigram, Major and Hon. Lieutenant-Colonel Banister Fletcher was promoted Lieutenant-Colonel with honorary rank of Colonel; he resigned 12th January, 1898.

Extract from Battalion Orders of 22nd January, 1898:

The Commanding Officer announces with very great regret the resignation of Colonel Banister Fletcher, V.D., J.P., D.L. Joining in June, 1867, Colonel Fletcher has passed through all the commission grades, always performing the duties required of him in a highly satisfactory manner. He has at all times given his valuable professional services for the advantage of the regiment, and will, in this particular, be remembered by the important additions and improvements carried out at the Headquarters under his experienced supervision.

Colonel Fletcher died 5th July, 1899.

Major Henry Coningham was promoted Lieutenant-Colonel, on Colonel Fletcher's retirement, resigning 22nd December, 1900.

Extract from Battalion Orders of 29th December, 1900:

In announcing the resignation of Colonel Henry Coningham, V.D., the Commanding Officer regrets deeply that he and the Battalion lose the services of an Officer who for over 20 years has worked hard to forward the best interests and efficiency of the Battalion, and has given him able and valued assistance as his second in command.

Major Vickers Dunfee was gazetted Lieutenant-Colonel; Captain E. V. Wellby becoming Major, 9th March, 1901.

Colonel Wigram died in July, 1894, and the following appeared in Battalion Orders 14th July, 1894 :—

> The Commanding Officer greatly regrets to hear of the death of Colonel Clifford Wigram, V.D. He served in the Brigade from April, 1860, to November, 1890, and during that thirty years did much for the Regiment, and since his retirement has continued to take a great interest in the Brigade. He will be much missed at its gatherings and his loss will be felt by all ranks.

Regulations were made in 1896 that Commanding Officers should hold their Command for four years only, all those then serving being considered as having been appointed in 1896. Colonel Wilde's term of command thus expired in November, 1900, when it was extended for a further two years, to 22nd November, 1902. His retirement appeared in District Orders, and the following was in Battalion Orders, 17th January, 1903:

EXTRACT FROM DISTRICT ORDERS.

> 1st (the Tower Hamlets Rifle Volunteer Brigade), Lieutenant-Colonel Commandant and Honorary Colonel E. T. Rodney Wilde, V.D., resigns his commission ; with permission to retain his rank and to wear the uniform of his Corps on retirement; dated 23rd November, 1902.
>
> The term of my command having expired, I would like on my retirement to express to the Officers, Non-Commissioned Officers and Members of the Tower Hamlets Rifle Brigade my very great appreciation of the earnest and ready manner in which my orders have at all times been carried out, and for the very valuable and warm-hearted assistance accorded to me in the affairs of the Battalion.
>
> I cannot help expressing my regret that the time has come for me to sever my connection with the Brigade, after an active service with it of forty-two years, but I trust I shall always have the pleasure of keeping up the valued friendships of all those who in the past as well as in the present have so earnestly worked with me.
>
> I shall continue to have the well-being of the Brigade always at heart, and feel sure it will maintain the excellent record it has so deservedly won.
>
> E. T. RODNEY WILDE,
> 24th November, 1902. Colonel.

Colonel Wilde's retirement did not appear in the *London Gazette* until 24th January, 1903. Colonel Vickers Dunfee was gazetted to command, 4th February, 1903.

Major E. V. Wellby became Lt.-Col., 14th February, 1903.

Guards of Honour have been furnished on many occasions, when Royalty and other distinguished personages have come to the district to lay foundation stones, open buildings, or perform other official functions.

The Annual Distribution of Prizes held at Headquarters and the Shoreditch Town Hall, usually in December, have been presided over by, amongst others : Lord Mayors, Mr. John Holmes, M.P., Lord Alfred Paget, Lady Abinger, Lord Harris, Lady Jane Taylor, Colonel Samuda, M.P., General Moncrieff (the Honorary Colonel), Colonel Holt, Colonel Stracey, Colonel Wigram, Colonel Gipps (Scots Guards), Mr. C. T. Ritchie, M.P., and the Officers Commanding the Home District and Brigade.

The Regiment has used the Ranges at Loughton, Ilford, Roxeth, Harrow, and Wormwood Scrubbs. In 1885 the Ilford range was closed for some time, and in consequence an extension of time for classing was allowed. Again in 1886 there was trouble about the ranges. The Battalion now goes to Pirbright for musketry.

When the Wimbledon Meetings were closed by a Review the T.H.R.V.B. always attended.

The T.H.R.V.B. was present at the Easter Monday Field Days each year, has furnished Detachments to the Easter Marching Columns, and supplied part of the Provisional Battalions formed for Camps at Aldershot, and has attended the Brigade Camps since their formation, and been present at all Musters of the Brigade to which it is attached.

The Regiment was present in Hyde Park on the occasion of the Royal Review by the Princess of Wales on 1st July, 1876, and at Windsor, 9th July, 1881, when the Queen reviewed the troops.

On 17th March, 1887, the Volunteer Regiments attached to the Scots Guards had a Route March from the City to the West End, under Lord Abinger, and on 9th June there was a Brigade Drill at Wimbledon with the Guards, Lord Abinger being in command, the troops proceeding to the Common by route march.

In January, 1885, Martini Henry Rifles were issued in place of the Snider. In December, 1896, Lee Metfords were received.

In 1887, the Battalion was stationed in Whitechapel Road, on the occasion of the visit of the Queen to the People's Palace, on 14th May; and it also took part in the march past at Buckingham Palace on 2nd July, and the Jubilee Review, at Aldershot, on 9th July.

On the 11th July, 1891, the Battalion, 620 strong, took part in the review held in honour of the German Emperor at Wimbledon.

In 1889 the Detachment in the Brigade Camp at Aldershot was joined by a further contingent on 7th August, and took part in the Field Day before the German Emperor.

In 1890 the Regiment received a grant from the Mansion House Patriotic Fund, raised by the Lord Mayor, Sir James Whitehead, Bart., with which it was enabled to purchase Slade Wallace Equipment for the total strength of the Battalion. The men paraded, fully equipped for the first time, on 11th October, 1890. The equipment consists of belts, straps, two pouches, great coat, haversack, mess tin and water bottle.

The Brigade attended the opening of the Tower Bridge on 30th June 1894 ; the Review by the Prince of Wales, 8th July, 1899 ; furnished a Detachment for the Diamond Jubilee 22nd June, 1897, when Major Locke as Officer in command received the Jubilee Medal ; also Detachments for the Coronation on 9th August, 1902 ; Captain Dade being in command received the Coronation Medal, which was also awarded to Colonel Wilde who commanded a Provisional Battalion, and to Captain Monson who acted as his Adjutant ; and a Detachment for the Royal Progress on 25th October, 1902.

On 1st March, 1902, military honours were paid to the remains of Lieutenant Norman Duncan-Teape who died on 25th February. The coffin was met by a Guard of Honour at

Waterloo Station on its conveyance to the country for burial. The following appeared in the Battalion Orders of 1st March, 1902 :—

> The Commanding Officer announces with extreme regret the death, on the 25th February, of Second Lieutenant N. Duncan-Teape, a most promising young Officer, who took the greatest interest in his duties.

A Church Parade has been held yearly, very frequently at St. Paul's Cathedral, but also at St. Botolph's, Bishopsgate Without, and St. John's, Hoxton, the Vicars—the Rev. W. Rogers and the Very Rev. G. P. Pownall—being Honorary Chaplains, and at St. Nicholas Cole Abbey, Queen Victoria Street, after the appointment of the Rector, the Rev. Professor H. C. Shuttleworth, in June, 1894. On his death in October, 1900, the following appeared in Battalion Orders on 3rd November, 1900 :—

> The Commanding Officer announces with extreme regret the death of the Chaplain, the Reverend Professor Shuttleworth, who showed his interest in the Battalion by his bright services so much appreciated at Church Parades.

The Rev. Edgar Sheppard, D.D., Sub-Dean of the Chapels Royal, and Sub-Almoner to the King was appointed Chaplain. He has held Church Parades at Christ Church, Newgate Street

In 1881 an Officers' Mess was established, the Officers dining together periodically ; at first at the " Horse Shoe," then for some years at the Café Royal, and now at the Hotel Cecil. There are at Headquarters a handsome ante-room, with dressing rooms, etc. The Mess possesses complete camp furniture for tents for thirty Officers.

The Officers have given very successful Dances from time to time ; one of the Mess Dinners is usually a Ladies' Evening.

The Officers have frequently taken part in the War Games played at the Home District Military Society, and have attended the outdoor exercises.

The Sergeants have a comfortable and convenient Mess Room at Headquarters ; they give very successful and pleasant Smokers, and Ladies' Evenings. An Annual Dinner is held at

Headquarters or at a City Restaurant. Having the necessary plant the Sergeants are able to make their own arrangements for messing when in camp. The Sergeants' Mess Room is sometimes used for Company Smokers.

The Sergeants have taken full advantage of the Membership of the Metropolitan Volunteer Sergeants' Tactical Association.

In August, 1882, Sergeant-Major Woodham, retiring after many years' service, Sergeant-Major Vance, formerly of the 8th King's Regiment, was appointed Sergeant-Major, and on his retirement, May, 1890, Sergeant-Instructor Monk, who was appointed Sergeant-Instructor from the Royal Marine Artillery in July, 1879, became Sergeant-Major. On his retirement in September, 1896, after 21 years' service in the Army and 17 years with the T.H.R.V.B., the following appeared in the Battalion Orders, 17th October, 1896 :—

> The Commanding Officer greatly regrets the retirement of Sergeant-Major C. Monk. During his seventeen years' service with the Corps, the Sergeant-Major has always performed his duties in a ready, thoroughly efficient and most satisfactory manner. The Commanding Officer feels he speaks for the Regiment as well as for himself in hoping that Sergeant-Major Monk may long enjoy the retirement which his nearly forty years' exemplary service so fully entitles him to.

Drill-Instructor and Colour-Sergeant George Dunkeld from the 1st Batt. Grenadier Guards was appointed Sergeant-Major.

On 28th September, 1895, a Military Funeral was given to Colour-Sergeant Bignell.

In March, 1901, Quarter-Master-Sergeant J. Towner retired, the following was in Battalion Orders of 2nd March, 1901 :—

> The Commanding Officer much regrets the retirement of Quarter-Master-Sergeant Towner, who has served in the Battalion for 40 years with an unvaryingly excellent record, always carrying out his duties to the complete satisfaction of his superiors; his performance of the important duty of Quarter-Master-Sergeant has earned him the grateful thanks of all for whom he has worked so long and so loyally.

In September, 1894, a new Lease of the Headquarters was granted by the freeholders for a term of sixty years.

Extensive additions, alterations, and repairs were made, at a total cost of £2,968 15s. 3d., under supervision of Colonel Banister Fletcher, V.D., J.P., F.R.I.B.A.

The Contractors were Messrs. Shepherd, who gave a pair of statuettes of past and present members, one in the uniform of 1803, and the other in that of 1893, for the overmantle.

In response to an appeal for assistance towards the heavy outlay incurred, the following contributions were received :—

The Corporation of London	... ...	£52	10 0
The Worshipful Company of Carpenters	... ...	52	10 0
,, ,,	Cutlers	10	10 0
,, ,,	Joiners	5	5 0
,, ,,	Leathersellers	52	10 0
,, ,,	Mercers	52	10 0
,, ,,	Merchant Taylors ...	10	10 0
,, ,,	Skinners	21	0 0
Mr. J. J. Griffiths, J.P. ...	... ...	5	5 0
Mr. C. F. Mills, J.P. ...	... ...	3	3 0
Mr. Newton	... ...	15	5 0

AMBULANCE.

The Regimental Bearer Detachment was organised in the beginning of 1876, by Surgeon-Major W. H. Platt, and was the first Volunteer Regimental Class formed ; it was inspected in the same year by Surgeon-General Munro, A.M.D., C.B., who passed high encomiums on its general smartness and efficiency.

The Detachment was raised with great difficulty, and was entirely a new departure ; it was only the untiring zeal, energy, and perseverance of the Medical Officers that overcame all obstacles and made it a strong and perfectly drilled body, and the pioneer and example for all other Volunteer Regimental Bearers. The Bearers were formed into a separate Command under the Medical Officers, as a section of a company, this arrangement working most satisfactorily. On Surgeon-Major Platt joining the Volunteer Medical Staff Corps in June, 1885,

Surgeon White, (who was appointed Brigade-Surgeon to the East London Volunteer Brigade, December, 1889), took up the active work. The Detachment has always been most efficient, and has passed well at each Annual Inspection, being highly complimented by the Army Medical Staff Officers. In May, 1890, an order was issued for the formation of a Bearer Company for the Brigade from members of the various Battalions.

In September, 1891, the Brigadier of the East London Volunteer Brigade, finding the scheme for each Corps to furnish a quota of men to the Brigade Ambulance was not satisfactory, ordered that a separate Brigade Bearer Company should be formed, and be on the strength of the T.H.R.V.B. Permission was granted for the Brigade Bearers to wear a Special Uniform, after the pattern of the Volunteer Medical Staff Corps, the braiding being white.

The complement of the Brigade Bearer Company was—

    1 Surgeon-Lieutenant-Colonel, or Surgeon-Major, or Surgeon-Captain.
    2 Surgeon-Captains or Surgeon-Lieutenants.
    7 Staff-Sergeants or Sergeants (Senior to act as Warrant Officer).
    1 Bugler.
    53 Rank and File.

Total 64 all Ranks.

The equipment consisted of—

    8 Stretchers.
    3 Surgical Haversacks.
    3 Water Bottles.
    1 Field Companion, completely fitted.
    1 Station Flag.
    4 Directing Flags.
    1 Field Hospital Red Lantern.
    2 Search Lanterns.

There was fixed in the Drill Hall a full-sized model of an Ambulance Waggon for drill purposes.

Blankets for carrying " wounded," and dust coats for " wounded " to lie down in, were among the stores.

In May, 1893, in response to an appeal by Mrs. Wilde, a very handsome Challenge Cup was subscribed for by the following ladies and presented, to be competed for by the Sections of the Brigade Bearer Company :—

Mrs. Abbott	Mrs. Moncrieff
Mrs. Coningham	Mrs. Money
Miss Coningham	Mrs. Pratt
Mrs. Dade	Mrs. Preston
Mrs. Davis	Hon. Mrs. Trotter
Miss Davis	Mrs. Thompson
Mrs. Ewer	Mrs. Ward
Miss Hilda Farish	Mrs. Waterhouse
Mrs. Fletcher	Mrs. White
Miss Froy	Mrs. Wilde
Miss Ferguson	Miss Wilde
Mrs. Harris	Mrs. Wright
Mrs. Locke	

The Cup is engraved :—

LADIES' CHALLENGE CUP, T.H.R.V.B.

PRESENTED TO

THE BEARER COMPANY, EAST LONDON VOLUNTEER BRIGADE, 1893.

It has been Won

In 1893 by Sergeant Bird's Section.
In 1894 by Sergeant Prior's Section.
In 1896 by Sergeant Scott's Section.

In February, 1897, an Ambulance Wagon, with tortoise tent, was purchased, and a Transport Section formed, trained in riding and driving; the wagon was on parade for the first time on Whit Monday of the same year and subsequently has attended Brigade Camps and other musters of the Brigade and the Battalion on special occasions.

Brigade-Surgeon Lieutenant-Colonel O. M. White, who had raised the Brigade Bearer Company and brought it to its satisfactory position, died on 2nd March, 1898. The following special order was issued on the 12th March, 1898 :—

DEATH.

The Commanding Officer with very great regret, in which he feels all ranks will join, announces the death, on the 2nd instant, of Brigade-Surgeon Lieutenant-Colonel O. M. White, Owing to his energy and perseverance the Brigade Bearer Company was formed, and it is due to his care and supervision that it has attained to the position it now occupies.

His death is a severe loss to the Regiment in which he took so deep an interest.

In the name of the Regiment the Commanding Officer offers deepest sympathy to the family of Surgeon-Colonel White in their heavy bereavement.

Subsequently the Commanding Officer notified the receipt of the following letter from Mrs. White :—

The Commanding Officer has received the following :—

Mrs. White wishes to convey to the Officers her heart-felt thanks for their kind sympathy, and feels very much their goodness in sending such lovely flowers. Her husband loved his soldiering and the T.H.R.B. so much that she trusts his memory may long remain green in the recollection of his old comrades.

In March, 1902, Brigade Bearer Companies were made separate units. A Company was raised for the 2nd London Volunteer Infantry Brigade, the T.H.R.V.B. finding Headquarters' accommodation. Many of the Members of the old East London Volunteer Brigade Bearer Company joined.

MACHINE GUN BATTERY.

In 1886 the Battery was formed by Captain Dunfee, and received two single-barrelled Gardner machine guns, one mounted on a field carriage and the other conveyed in a hand cart. The battery with this armament was with the Easter Marching Column under Colonel, now General, Moncrieff that year. The second gun was soon mounted on a field carriage and two limbers built ; after some difficulty, as machine guns were not then allowed as part of the equipment of an infantry battalion, the Battery was permitted to parade with the Brigade for inspection in 1887. In 1888 the two single-barrelled guns were exchanged for those with double barrels ; in the next year the limbers had single barrels mounted on them, so that there was then a battery of four guns. Early in 1890 a third double-barrelled weapon was added, with its limber and single-barrel gun, and thus the Battery was complete with six guns.

Since 1886, some of the guns have always been with the Easter Marching Columns, and at the Brigade Camps at Aldershot.

The Battery has taken part in the display of all arms at the Royal Military Tournaments at the Agricultural Hall.

The Battery first turned out with the six guns at Folkestone, Easter, 1890, under Colonel Stracey, Scots' Guards.

As the ordinary uniform was found to be unsuited to the work, a special outfit was provided in 1888, somewhat similar to the dress of Mounted Infantry, consisting of a scarlet kersey, corduroy breeches and puttees. The men are fully equipped and carry also spades and axes, the rifles being conveyed on the gun carriages and limbers. The guns are hauled by drag ropes and straps passed over the shoulder for manœuvreing, but on the line of march by a horse for each gun and limber.

The Battery consists of—
- Three double-barrelled Gardner Guns mounted on Field Carriages.
- Three Limbers, having a single-barrelled Gardner Gun on each.
- Ammunition Boxes, two on each Field Carriage, carrying together 1,250 rounds, and the two on each Limber 3,000 rounds.

Machine Guns are now allowed for Infantry Battalions.

The carriages and limbers with shafts now in use have been perfected with a great deal of trouble and expense.

At the Annual Inspection in Hyde Park on 9th July, 1892, the Battery appeared for the first time with horses, shafts being fitted to each limber, so that one horse drew a limber and gun ; three led horses being required for the full Battery.

In July, 1896, the barrels were altered to ·303 at considerable expense ; a tripod stand designed by Captain Dunfee was brought into use.

In 1893 a very handsome Challenge Cup was presented to the Battery.

The T.H.R.V.B. was greatly indebted to the Gardner Gun Company in reference to this Battery.

Very satisfactory practice has been made with ball cartridge when the Battery has had the opportunity of firing at Hythe and Aldershot.

The Machine Gun Detachment of Maxims which went out to South Africa with the C.I.V.'s was furnished chiefly from the Machine Gun Battery of the T.H.R.V.B., under command of Captain E. V. Wellby, who held the rank of Lieutenant. The Maxims Detachment earned for itself great commendation; Lieutenant Wellby was mentioned in Dispatches, and Sergeant W. J. Park received the Distinguished Conduct Medal.—*Gazette* of 27th September, 1901.

On the return of the C.I.V., the men of the Machine Gun Battery dragged their four guns through London, although horses had been sent to Paddington to meet them.

These Maxim guns were placed for the time under the care of the T.H.R.V.B., and exhibited at the Military Exhibition at Earl's Court in 1901.

The following notice was put up over the guns :—

C.I.V. MACHINE GUNS.

These were used throughout the campaign with the Regiment, and took part in the following engagements :—Dornkop, Little Spitzkop, Donkers Poort, Roadebergen, Diamond Hill, Stephanus Draai.

At Diamond Hill Sergeant Stevens (R.F.A.) who was in charge of the Infantry Section, was the only one to bring a Machine Gun into action during the engagement.

During the several days' fighting just previous to the surrender of General Prinsloo, the guns were frequently used, on one occasion causing a 15-pounder Boer gun to retire.

The Detachments were drawn from the Machine Gun Battery 1st Tower Hamlets V.R.C., to which Regiment the guns are to be entrusted for safe keeping.

The Diploma of Honour—the highest possible award—was awarded to the exhibit of the guns.

When the Maxims were released from the Exhibition, Sir Alfred Newton, Bart., in whose Mayoralty the C.I.V. were raised, wished to present the guns to the T.H.R.V.B., but great difficulties arose, and it was only with the assistance of the Hon. Claude Hay, M.P. for Hoxton, and others interested, that the kind intentions of Sir Alfred Newton were at last carried out, the guns having been first put into a thorough state of repair.

The Regiment is particularly gratified for these historic guns to be entrusted to its care.

The following appeared in the Battalion Orders of 14th June, 1902 :—

> The Commanding Officer is glad to announce that he has received permission to accept the four Maxim Machine Guns of the late C.I.V., which were worked by Non-Commissioned Officers and men of the Battalion in South Africa, under Major Wellby, kindly offered by Sir Alfred J. Newton, Bart.

The following Inscription is on the Maxim Guns :—

> This Gun, together with its carriage, is one of four forming part of the equipment presented by the Corporation of the City of London to the City Imperial Volunteers, on the formation of that Corps, A.D. 1900. These four guns served with the Corps during the Campaign in South Africa against the Boers, and after the disbandment of the Battalion were handed over by Sir Alfred J. Newton, Bart. (Lord Mayor, 1899-1900), to the Secretary of State for War, on behalf of the Corporation of the City of London.

On receipt of the Maxims, the single-barrel Gardners were removed from the Limbers and one Field Gun dispensed with, that the battery of six Machine Guns might be worked on a principle similar to Royal Field Artillery.

The Machine Guns are stored in a convenient shed in the Drill Hall, and with the harness and appliances, very carefully looked after, the excellent condition in which all is maintained reflecting the greatest credit on the Members of the Battery.

CYCLISTS.

The Section was formed in August, 1894; has done much useful work when the Battalion has been out for field days, etc., and has taken part in the Cycling operations of the Brigade.

The Cyclists have attended the Brigade Camps at Aldershot, Chatham, Colchester and Yarmouth, a large muster proceeding by road under the command of Colour-Sergeant J. Harrison.

SIGNALLING.

A complete Signalling Equipment is at Headquarters, consisting of eighteen large and eight small flags, four lanterns and stands and two heliographs with stands and a telescope. Some of the men are trained in their use, and have furnished Stations on marching columns and other occasions.

In June, 1892, Captain H. E. Davis took charge of the Signallers and was appointed Acting Brigade Signalling Officer, 30th January, 1895, resigning the appointment in November, 1895, and his commission on 4th December, 1895.

Lieutenant H. T. Barnett who passed in Signalling, 20th December, 1897, was appointed Brigade Signalling Officer 1st April, 1898; he resigned on 18th October, 1898.

Captain I. Cohen passed in Signalling 4th March, 1902, and was appointed Captain Commanding Brigade Signalling Company, 2nd London Volunteer Infantry Brigade, 14th April, 1902.

SHOOTING.

As already mentioned the Brigade has used various ranges, most of them however not favourable for long distance shooting.

Representatives have entered for the Queen's, St. George's, and other N.R.A. Competitions, and teams for the "Daily Telegraph" Cup, and Dewar Shield; matches have been fired from time to time with other Battalions and Regimentally.

Field firing has been performed in Camp at Aldershot and on the Pirbright Ranges, and judging distances carried out as opportunity offered.

The arrangements for the various Competitions and Prizes are made by the Shooting Committee who have also the duty of raising the funds required to provide for the long list of Prizes presented at the Annual Distribution.

In the Drill Hall there is a Morris Tube Range used for training recruits and practice, a Club being attached to the Range.

Captain Briscoe obtained a Hythe Certificate, 27th April, 1898, and was appointed Instructor of Musketry, 25th May, 1898, resigning on 23rd April, 1902, when Captain Cohen, who obtained his Certificate 18th October, 1900, was appointed.

We may mention that Captain Cohen has patented an instrument for teaching aiming, which has received the warm praise of the Military Authorities and all those who are interested in this important part of a soldier's training.

SERGEANTS IN POSSESSION OF HYTHE CERTIFICATES.

Armourer-Sergeant Testi, G. C.	17th November, 1900
Colour-Sergeant McAdam, A.	4th July, 1902
Sergeant-Inst. Musketry Bryant, T.	10th May, 1901
Colour-Sergeant Langdon, Alfred R.	14th April, 1903
Sergeant Millard, A. W.	4th July, 1902

THE HOLMES CHALLENGE CUP.

Presented to the " Tower Hamlets Rifle Volunteer Brigade," the " First Administrative Battalion of the Tower Hamlets," the " 6th Tower Hamlets," and the " 9th Essex " Rifle Volunteer Corps, by

JOHN HOLMES, M.P.

The " First Administrative Battalion of the Tower Hamlets " is now the " Second Tower Hamlets Volunteer Rifle Corps "; the " Sixth Tower Hamlets " is absorbed in the T.H.R.V.B.; the " Ninth Essex Rifle Volunteer Corps " is now the " Fourth Volunteer Battalion of the Essex Regiment." The Competition has been annually since September, 1873, under rules approved by Mr. Holmes, 18th August, 1873, and the T.H.R.V.B. has been very successful.

The names of the winning Corps are engraved on the Cup as follows :

1873	...	9th Essex R.V.	1889 ...	T.H.R.V.B.
1874	...	T.H.R.V.B.	1890 ...	2nd T.H.R.V.C.
1875	...	,,	1891 ...	,,
1876	...	,,	1892 ...	T.H.R.V.B.
1877	...	9th Essex R.V.	1893 ...	,,
1878	...	T.H.R.V.B.	1894 ...	2nd T.H.R.V.C.
1879	...	,,	1895 ...	T.H.R.V.B.
1880	...	,,	1896 ...	Tie { T.H.R.V.B. / 2nd T.H.R.V.C.
1881	...	,,		
1882	...	,,	1897 ...	T.H.R.V.B.
1883	...	,,	1898 ...	,,
1884	...	Not fired for	1899 ...	4th V.B. Essex
1885	...	T.H.R.V.B.	1900 ...	,,
1886	...	,,	1901 ...	,,
1887	...	,,	1902 ...	,,
1888	...	2nd T.H.R.V.C.		

The Battalion possesses several handsome and valuable Challenge Prizes, besides the Cups belonging to different Companies.

The Battalion Challenge Cup.

This large handsome Silver Cup, weighing 112 ozs., was originally presented to the North-East London Rifles for individual competition. The winner receives a purse and a photograph of the cup, and has his name engraved on the cup.

It has been won in—

1864	by Sergeant H. Walker	1884	by Sergt. W. White
1865	,, Q.M.-Sergt. S. Partrick	1885	,, Pte. W. Bullimore
1866	,, Col.-Sergt. C. Hum	1886	,, Sergt. W. White
1867	,, Sergt. C. Rance	1887	,, Pte. E. Tempest
1868	,, } Not recorded.	1888	,, Pte. J. Curnow
1869	,,	1889	,, Pte. J. Curnow
1870	,, Col.-Sergt. J. Towner	1890	,, Pte. J. Curnow
1871	,, Col.-Sergt. J. Towner	1891	,, Col.-Sergt. J. Towner
1872	,, Cpl. E. Butler	1892	,, Q.-M.-Sergt. J. Towner
1873	,, Sergt. H. Noble	1893	,, Pte. D. McClusky
1874	,, Pte. E. Tempest	1894	,, Cpl. S. Adams
1875	,, Sergt. J. Sage	1895	,, Pte. J. Curnow
1876	,, Pte. J. Curnow	1896	,, Pte. W. Clapp
1877	,, Sergt. J. Sage	1897	,, Q.-M.-Sergt. J. Towner
1878	,, Pte. S. Adams	1898	,, Pte. W. Clapp
1879	,, Pte. W. C. Bullimore	1899	,, Sergt. W. Seal
1880	,, Sgt. J. Sage	1900	,, Col.-Sergt. C. Warren
1881	,, Capt. T. Smith	1901	,, Pnr.-Sergt. A. Rampling
1882	,, Cpl. W. Arle	1902	,, Pnr.-Sergt. A. Rampling
1883	,, Sergt. J. Sage		

The Thomson Shield.

The inscription on this is as follows :—

In Memoriam
TO THE LATE
LIEUTENANT-COLONEL JAMES THOMSON,
Who commanded the Tower Hamlets Rifle Brigade.
Died June 8th, 1870.

THIS SHIELD

Was subscribed for by the Members of the above Corps to be shot for annually by Squads of Companies of the Tower Hamlets Rifle Volunteer Brigade.

The Winners are inscribed on silver plates on the frame as follows:

Year	Company		Year	Company	
1874	... J	Company	1889	... L	Company
1875	... L	,,	1890	... L	,,
1876	... L	,,	1891	... L	,,
1877	... J	,,	1892	... L	,,
1878	... L	,,	1893	... L	,,
1879	... D	,,	1894	... L	,,
1880	... M	,,	1895	... L	,,
1881	... L	,,	1896	... L	,,
1882	... L	,,	1897	... L	,,
1883	... L	,,	1898	... L	,,
1884	... L	,,	1899	... L	,,
1885	... L	,,	1900	... L	,,
1886	... L	,,	1901	... L	,,
1887	... L	,,	1902	... L	,,
1888	... L	,,			

THE PHILHARMONIC CUP

was presented by Messrs. Turner & Adams for competition between the 6th Tower Hamlets and the 39th Middlesex. It was won by the first-named corps in 1866, and is now a Regimental Challenge Cup.

Up to 1890 it was fired for by Companies, since then by individuals.

As far as recorded the winners have been :—

Year	Winner	Year	Winner
1877	... D Company	1891	... Col.-Sergt. Tottle
1878	... L ,,	1892	... Sergt. Rampling
1879	... Not recorded	1893	... Pte. J. Crick
1880	... L Company	1894	... ,, E. Tempest
1881	... Not recorded	1895	... ,, J. Crick
1882	... D Company	1896	... ,, E. Tempest
1883	... L ,,	1897	... Pnr.-Sergt. Rampling
1884	... L ,,	1898	... Pnr.-Sergt. Rampling
1885	... L ,,	1899	... Sergt. G. Couch
1886	... L ,,	1900	... Col.-Sergt. W. Nathan
1887	... L ,,	1901	... Corpl. F. Child
1888	... L ,,	1902	... Q.-M.-Sergt. Warren
1889	... L ,,		
1890	... L ,,		

D

First Clapton Cup.

A Silver Cup weighing 26 ozs. presented to the First Corps by the Ladies of Clapton in 1870, is a Regimental Challenge Cup carrying a purse to the winner.

The names of the winners as far as recorded have been :—

1870 ...	Sergt. A. Mills	1890 ...	Col.-Sergt. White
1874 ...	,, H. T. Hurst	1891 ...	,, J. Towner
1877 ...	Pte. J. Curnow	1892 ...	Pte. Bullimore
1878 ...	,, J. Curnow	1893 ... Tie	{ Pte. E. Tempest
1880 ...	Sergt. Sage		{ ,, W. Clapp
1881 ...	Capt. Smith	1894 ...	O.-R.-Sergt. W. White
1882 ...	Pte. H. Sage	1895 ...	Pte. J. Curnow
1883 ...	Sergt. W. Clapp	1896 ...	Sergt. W. Seal
1884 ...	Cpl. Rookesley	1897 ...	,, W. L. Nathan
1885 ...	Sergt. Clapp	1898 ...	Pte. W. Clapp
1886 ...	Cpl. Arle	1899 ...	,, A. Fowell
1887 ...	,, Adams	1900 ...	,, W. Sage
1888 ...	Col.-Sergt. Tasker	1901 ...	,, R. Bullimore
1889 ...	,, Tasker	1902 ...	Sergt. L. Seal

Second Clapton Cup.

A Silver Cup, presented to the Second Corps in September, 1871, by Captain Gibbs, is now a Regimental Challenge Cup carrying a purse to the winner.

The names of the winners have not been engraved on the Cup each year. The names recorded are :—

1871 ...	Cpl. F. Priest	1892 ...	Pte. W. Seal
1880 ...	Pte. E. Tempest	1893 ... Tie	{ Pte. McClusky
1881 ...	,, S. Adams		{ Q.-M. Sergt. Towner
1882 ...	Col.-Sergt. Costin	1894 ...	Pte. W. Sage
1883 ...	Pte. J. Curnow	1895 ...	,, E. Tempest
1884 ...	,, J. Shaw	1896 ...	O.R. Sergt. W. White
1885 ...	Capt. Smith	1897 ...	Pte. Bullimore
1886 ...	Sergt. Home	1898 ...	Sergt. W. Seal
1887 ...	Col.-Sergt. Costin	1899 ...	Col.-Sergt. C. Warren
1888 ...	Pte. E. Tempest	1900 ...	Pte. W. Clapp
1889 ...	,, J. Curnow	1901 ...	Pnr.-Sergt. Rampling
1890 ...	,, E. Tempest	1902 ...	Pnr.-Sergt. Rampling
1891 ...	Col.-Sergt. Costin		

The Quartermaster's Cup.

In September, 1894, Captain and Quarter-Master C. Davis and a few friends presented a handsome Silver Challenge Vase for annual competition. It has been competed for on conditions very similar to those of the "Daily Telegraph" Cup.

Winning Companies have been :—

				Commander of Team
1894	...	L Company	...	Colour-Sergeant Mathias
1895	...	L ,,	...	Lieutenant W. V. Ward
1896	...	G ,,	...	,, Briscoe
1897	...	L ,,	...	,, W. V. Ward
1898	...	L ,,	...	,, Waterfield
1899	...	L ,,	...	,, W. V. Ward
1900	...	G ,,	...	Captain E. C. Harris
1901	...	L ,,	...	Lieutenant S. R. Abbott
1902	...	M ,,	...	,, S. Moore

In 1901, Lieutenant-Colonel Wellby presented the Sergeants' Mess with a handsome Challenge Shield to be shot for annually by the Sergeants of the T.H.V.R.B.

Winners—

1901 ... Sergt.-Instr. C. Jones   1902 ... Sergt. W. Seal

The Claude Hay Challenge Cup.

In December, 1901, The Hon. Claude Hay, M.P. for the Hoxton Division of Shoreditch, wrote Colonel Wilde the following letter :—

" 30, Throgmorton Street,
" E.C.
" 2nd December, 1901.

" Dear Colonel Wilde,

" I have been thinking over how I could best show my
" appreciation of the compliment paid to me by your Regiment,
" which I have for long admired, in enrolling me as Honorary
" Member of the Corps.

" The efficiency of the 1st Tower Hamlets V.R.C. is a
" household word throughout London, and my natural impulse is
" to try and devise some incentive whereby that efficiency can be
" extended to even greater numbers. Subject, therefore, to your
" approval, I beg to offer for your acceptance a " Claude Hay "
" Challenge Cup, upon the conditions set out below,

"I need not assure you of the great pleasure with which
"I make this offer, and I much hope that opportunities will arise
"when I may be enabled to be of some service to a Corps which is
"a noble example of the Volunteer Movement in the Metropolis.
"Believe me to be,
"Yours very truly,
"CLAUDE G. HAY.
"COL. E. T. RODNEY WILDE, V.D.,
"Commanding T.H.R.B."

RULES.

1.—The Cup and Money Prizes are open to all Members of the Regiment. The winner's name is to be inscribed on the Cup.

2.—Recruits counting for this Competition must be Efficient by 31st October in the year òf enrolment.

3.—Recruits joining the Army, and who are Efficient, will count for this Competition.

4.—Ties will be decided by the aggregate number of Drills performed by the Recruits Efficient.

PRIZES.

First Prize, the Cup and Photograph and £1 10s. to the Member who brings in the largest number of Recruits; second prize, £1 5s.; third prize, 17s. 6d.; fourth prize, 12s. 6d.; fifth prize, 10s.; sixth prize, 5s.

Winners, 1902.

1	Colour-Sergeant T. Bryant	K	Company.
2	Battery-Sergeant Major C. Winkworth	M	,,
3	Colour-Sergeant F. Rudman	F	,,
4	Colour-Sergeant D. L. Nathan	D	,,
5	Lance-Corporal W. H. Turner	B	,,
6	Lance-Corporal J. W. How	B	,,

The Battalion has a handsome Silver Bugle, mounted as an ornament for the Mess Table, which bears the inscription :—

"Presented by the Ladies of Poplar to the 4th and 5th Companies, Tower Hamlets Rifles, June 26th, 1861."

A new nominal Roll was prepared on 1st January, 1874, of the 1006 Officers, Non-Commissioned Officers and Men then serving in the Amalgamated Corps.

On the 31st December, 1902, there were still serving of those whose names were on the above Roll :—

    No. 63   Colonel E. T. Rodney Wilde
    ,, 264   Armourer-Sergeant J. Tasker
    ,, 374   Private J. Curnow
    ,, 517   ,,   W. Sage

The last number on the Roll on 31st December, 1902, was 7076, so that 6070 have joined the T.H.R.V.B. since 1st January, 1874.

Colonel Wilde retired 24th January, 1903.

Staff-Armourer Sergeant Tasker resigned 14th April, 1903, when the following order was issued :—

    The Commanding Officer much regrets the retirement of Staff Armourer-Sergeant Tasker, who has served in the Battalion for over 36 years with an unvaryingly excellent record, always carrying out his duties to the complete satisfaction of his superiors.

Volunteer Officers' Decoration.

Instituted 25th July, 1892.

The following Officers have received this :

    Lieut.-Col. and Hon. Col. E. T. Rodney Wilde
    Lieut.-Col. and Hon. Col. Banister Fletcher
    Lieut.-Col. and Hon. Col. Henry Coningham
    Major and Hon. Lieut.-Col. J. S. Thompson
    Major and Hon. Lieut.-Col. J. E. Ewer
    Major and Hon. Lieut.-Col. A. C. Preston
    Captain and Hon.-Major Locke
        (Who had already received the Volunteer Long Service Medal).
    Captain and Hon. Major Henry Wright

The following Officers who had retired prior to 1892 also received the decoration :—

    Lieut.-Col. and Hon. Col. Clifford Wigram
    Major and Hon. Lieut.-Col. J. de la Mare
    Major and Hon. Lieut.-Col. T. Smith
    Surgeon-Major J. H. Paul
    Hon. Major Armar Lowry
    Surgeon-Lieut.-Col. T. Gray

The following Non-Commissioned Officers and Men have received the Volunteer Long Service Medal (instituted 1894):

Qr.-Mr.-Sergt. G. Heron	Lce.-Cpl. H. Hemmings
Armr-Sergt. J. G. Tasker	,, J. Waite
Qr.-Mr. Sergt. J. Towner	Pioneer R. Bullimore
Batt.-Sgt.-Maj. C. T. Winkworth	Drummer F. Desbois
Col.-Sergt. H. Balls	Bugler F. Denyer
,, W. Burt	,, G. A. W. Merner
,, R. W. Church	,, W. Rayment
,, T. G. Costin	Private G. Barker
,, A. Ellis	,, W. G. Barns
,, H. Forster	,, J. Crick
,, H. T. Garrett	,, H. A. Crossley
,, J. W. Knights	,, W. Clapp
,, J. Lucombe	,, J. Curnow
,, G. Mathias	,, R. Curson
,, D. L. Nathan	,, W. H. Dawson
,, H. J. Noble	,, H. Elder
,, C. J. Poole	,, A. Fowell
,, T. Powley	,, G. Frewer
,, J. Tottle	,, G. Gladwell
,, T. Watson	,, A. Green
Sergeant-Bugler F. J. E. Merner	,, G. B. Gregory
Sergeant G. W. Ayres	,, C. Harvie
,, G. Couch	,, W. T. Hitchcock
,, E. Erwood	,, W. S. Hudson
,, G. Hammersley	,, C. D. Hum
,, G. Minchin	,, W. Lee
,, G. Newson	,, J. Lewington
,, W. J. J. Platt	,, J. E. May
,, A. Prior	,, M. Pelman
,, J. Tillman	,, H. Oxenham
,, G. Riddle	,, G. Penn
,, S. G. Shearmur	,, W. Rawson
,, R. Suter	,, A. Sage
Corporal S. Adams	,, W. Sage
,, E. Butler	,, W. Shaw
,, J. Merrick	,, J. Stanley
,, T. J. Morgan	,, J. Stevens
,, W. E. Withyman	,, S. Tarrant
,, (Pioneer) W. Verrall	,, E. Tempest
Lce.-Cpl. H. J. Barltrop	,, J. Williams

ACTIVE SERVICE.

In the Battalion Orders of 23rd December, 1899, Volunteers were called for the City of London Imperial Volunteers, raised by the Lord Mayor, Sir Alfred J. Newton, to be equipped at the expense of the City.

The Battalion Orders of 6th January, 1900, contains the names of four Sergeants, one Bugler, and twenty-eight Rank and File, who had been accepted for service. On the 8th January, 1900, Captain Wellby was gazetted Lieutenant in the C.I.V., and to have command of the Maxim Machine Gun Section to work the four guns, for which he selected men from his own M Company, the Machine Gun Company of the T.H.R.V.B. On 13th January, a "send off" was given at Headquarters and each man presented with a pipe and a tin of tobacco. A Draft of re-inforcement of twelve Non-Commissioned Officers and men went out on 12th July, 1900.

The 29th October, 1900, saw the return of the C.I.V., when the Battalion was on duty in Cheapside with the view of keeping the road clear, rendered, however, quite impossible by the immense crowds gathered to see the troops pass on their way to the Guildhall, and the Honourable Artillery Company's Headquarters, where they were entertained by the City of London.

On the 3rd November, the Members of the C.I.V. were entertained at Dinner by the Officers at the Metropolitan Hotel in the City, and afterwards conveyed in Omnibuses to Headquarters where a great reception awaited them.

The four Maxim Machine Guns were left in charge at Headquarters till they were taken to the Exhibition at Earl's Court in April, 1901, and after much trouble and delay, the

Guns have been handed over to the T.H.R.V.B., Sir Alfred J. Newton, Bart. desiring they should continue with the Battalion, who supplied the men to work them.

We append Nominal Rolls of those who joined the C.I.V. and the re-inforcing draft :—

NOMINAL ROLL

OF THE ONE OFFICER AND THIRTY-EIGHT NON-COMMISSIONED OFFICERS AND MEN OF THE

TOWER HAMLETS RIFLE VOLUNTEER BRIGADE WHO JOINED THE CITY OF LONDON IMPERIAL VOLUNTEERS.

Captain E. V. Wellby, as Lieutenant in Command of Machine Gun Section.

Sergeant J. Blatt
,, W. J. Park
,, R. G. Richards
Corporal H. J. Bowden
,, W. G. Clerke
,, T. Dyer
Lance-Corporal E. G. Burrell
,, A. E. Farley
,, F. Patten
,, C. Sheen
Bugler G. Hardy
Private C. R. Ayres
,, T. Cooper
,, T. W. Cotter
,, H. Curtis
,, A. Day
,, C. J. Day
,, P. Glassey
,, J. J. Hall
Private C. Halls
,, C. R. Hanham
,, A. Hatley
,, A. Lindsell
,, A. E. McKewan
,, W. D. Roberts
,, J. Say
,, A. Smart
,, A. W. A. Stroud
,, E. Susands
,, E. Travers
,, J. Tyndale
,, W. Walker
,, W. A. Walker
,, G. Walliss
,, H. G. Warren
,, T. W. Wells
,, G. Wild
,, J. W. Willsher

THE RE-INFORCING DRAFT

Consisted of the following eleven Non-commissioned Officers and Men, who sailed 12th July, 1900.

Coporal P. W. Crowson
Lance-Corporal W. H. Glibbery
Private R. W. Daniell
,, H. H. Dorrington
,, A. E. Heaford
,, H. E. Jones
Private F. L. Jordan
,, A. A. Pateman
,, A. F. Richardson
,, A. V. Strike
,, T. Sweetingham

Private C. J. Day was killed in action at Frederickstad, 31st July, 1900.

Corporal T. Dyer, died at Heilbrom, 3rd June, 1900, of enteric; Privates P. Glassey, died at Naauwpoort, 7th June, 1900, of enteric; J. Say, died at Pretoria, 23rd September, 1900, of enteric; J. Tyndale, died of disease; W. A. Walker died at the Orange River, 5th April, 1900, of dysentry; and G. Walliss died at Florida, in June, 1900, of enteric; seven were invalided home; one was left sick in South Africa; A. Smart joined the South African Police; and the other thirty-five of the forty-nine who went out returned with the C.I.V., in October, 1900.

Lieutenant E. V. Wellby, was mentioned in dispatches.

Sergeant W. J. Park received the distinguished conduct medal, 27th September, 1901.

The war medal with four and five clasps was issued to all.

Memorial Tablets with suitable inscriptions in memory of those who died on Service have been affixed in Churches, as under :—

To Private C. J. Day, St. Leonard's, Shoreditch
,,   T. Dyer, St. Thomas, Bethnal Green
,,   P. Glassey, Parish Church of Lower Edmonton
,,   J. Say, St. Leonard's, Shoreditch
,,   J. Tyndale, St. Bartholomew-in-the-East
,,   W. A. Walker, St. Lawrence, Jewry
,,   G. Walliss, St. Luke's, E.C.

In addition to those who joined the C.I.V., the following also served in South Africa :—

Captain J. L. Coakley, Vol. Service Co., Kings Royal Rifles
Lieutenant L. J. Stephenson (Local Captain), Vol. Service Co., Oxford Light Infantry
Sergeant Andrews, Imperial Yeomanry
,,   J. A. Brady   ,,
,,   Butler   ,,
,,   A. E. Langdon   ,,
,,   J. G. Lapthorne   ,,
Corporal S. J. Dunn   ,,
,,   E. W. Lappidge, R.A.M.C.
Lance-Corporal E. G. Burrell, Imperial Yeomanry
,,   L. L. Longley   ,,
,,   A. Lowde   ,,
,,   A. F. Richardson   ,,
,,   Turner   ,,

Bugler C. Rowe, Imperial Yeomanry
Private G. Allen, Royal Reserve
,, J. Bailey, Imperial Yeomanry
,, W. Barnes ,,
,, A. Bottomley ,,
,, H. J. Bright ,,
,, E. Campion ,,
,, W. Clamp ,,
,, W. J. Cochrane, Volunteer Service Co., King's Royal Rifles
,, D. Conway, Imperial Yeomanry
,, A. H. Corbett, ,,
,, Doo, South African Constabulary
,, J. Dormer, Imperial Yeomanry
,, R. Dumble, R.A.M.C.
,, A. Ely, Imperial Yeomanry
,, J. W. Fletcher ,,
,, R. Flook ,,
,, A. Garrard ,,
,, A. W. Green, R.A.M.C.
,, J. Haines, Imperial Yeomanry
,, E. Hargreaves, Sharp Shooters
,, G. Hilling, Imperial Yeomanry
,, C. Hodges ,,
,, S. King, Sharp Shooters
,, J. E. Lagden, Imperial Yeomanry
,, Lawings, South African Constabulary
,, Long, Imperial Yeomanry
,, T. B. Louder ,,
,, W. J. Luckie, South African Light Horse
,, Manson, R.A.M.C.
,, Manuel, Imperial Yeomanry
,, J. Marsh ,,
,, J. E. Moulding, Royal Reserve
,, H. Moffatt, Imperial Yeomanry
,, T. Newsham ,,
,, R. H. Noble ,,
,, H. R. Oldfield ,,
,, A. Purkiss ,,
,, B. Ritchie, Sharp Shooters
,, Samuels, Imperial Yeomanry
,, J. J. Sease ,,
,, C. E. Smith ,,
,, T. Stamford ,,
,, H. Towler ,,
,, W. Waddington ,,
,, J. T. Webb ,,
,, W. H. Whatcoat ,,
,, A. E. White ,,
,, J. Wright ,,

On the disbandment of the C.I.V., Lance-Corporal C. Sheen joined the Peninsular Horse, and later the Australian Bushmen ; Lance-Corporal E. G. Burrell and Bugler Hardy the Imperial Yeomanry.

Several Ex-officers of the Brigade served in South Africa.

Major Parr, Captain in the 18th Battalion Imperial Yeomanry.

Lieutenant J. Slaughter, Lieutenant in 3rd Battalion Imperial Yeomanry.

Lieutenant R. J. A. T. Slaughter, Second Lieutenant in South Lancashire Regiment.

Lieutenant C. C. Stuart, Lieutenant in the 1st Battalion Manchester Regiment.

Lieutenant A. E. B. Hovelt was attached to the King's Royal Rifles Depot, and served as Lieutenant in the 14th Provincial Battalion at Cork.

A list of the Officers and Sergeants serving on the 7th May, 1903, is furnished. (See page 61.)

We give the Annual Returns from 1874 to 1891, and fuller returns on to 1902, they are made up to 31st October in each year. It is to be noticed that the T.H.R.V.B. reached its greatest strength at the time of the operations in Egypt, during 1884-6, and the war in South Africa in 1900.

We have made up a Return of the Officers who were in the T.H.R.V.B. on the 1st January, 1874, and who have joined since that date, and had retired up to 7th May, 1903. There are 142 names. (See page 71.)

We also give the names and dates of the services of the retired Adjutants and Sergeant-Majors. (See page 78.)

It will fully recompense us for the time and trouble devoted to what has been a very pleasant task, if the particulars we have put together are found to be of interest to those who are now serving, as well as those who have retired from the T.H.R.V.B.

We must express our best thanks to all who have so kindly assisted us in our work, by furnishing information and looking over the proofs.

CHANGE OF DESIGNATION.

D.O., No. 105, 8th May, 1903.

It is notified for information that His Majesty, the King has been graciously pleased to approve of the 1st Tower Hamlets Volunteer Rifle Corps being in future designated the 4th Volunteer Battalion, the Royal Fusiliers (City of London Regiment).

Authority :—War Office letter, No. V/10/94/238, dated 30/4/1903.

The Tower Hamlets Rifle Volunteer Brigade consequently ceased on 7th May, 1903, and this history fitly closes on that date.

We can only wish the old Regiment every and continued success under its new designation.

There is an Appendix, giving a Diary of Events.

At special request the Author has given his personal reminiscences.

An Index will be found at end of the book.

THE TOWER HAMLETS RIFLE VOLUNTEER BRIGADE.

OFFICERS SERVING ON 7TH MAY, 1903.

‡ Active Service.
p.s. Passed School of Instruction.   *p.* Certificate of Proficiency.
t. Passed in Tactics.   *T.* Special Mention in Tactics.
H. Qualified for Appointment as Instructor in Musketry.
S. Certificate as Instructor in Army Signalling.

Hon. Colonel:

‡MONCRIEFF, G. H., Lieutenant-General ...   24th July, 1886.
   Ensign, 1st Foot, 6th June, 1854.
   Ensign and Lieutenant, Scots Guards, 4th August, 1854.
   Lieutenant and Captain, 15th January, 1856.
   Captain and Lieutenant-Colonel, 19th August, 1862.
   Lieutenant-Colonel, 1st July, 1881.
   Colonel, 1st April, 1887.
   Major-General, 31st December, 1887.
   Lieutenant-General, 1st April, 1895.
   Assistant Military Secretary, Headquarters of Army, 1st April, 1887, to 30th March, 1890.
   Brigadier-General, Curragh Brigade, 1st April, 1890, to 30th April, 1891.
   Major-General, Dublin District, 1st May, 1891, to 31st March, 1895.

Lieutenant-Colonel Commandant:

DUNFEE, V. (*p.s.*), (*t.*) ... ...   14th February, 1903.
   Lieutenant, 6th September, 1884.
   Captain, 3rd August, 1889.
   Major, 15th December, 1897.
   Lieutenant-Colonel, 2nd January, 1901.

Lieutenant-Colonel :

‡WELLBY, E. V. (*p.s.*) (*t.*)... ... 4th February, 1903.
    Second Lieutenant, 18th September, 1895.
    Lieutenant, 16th December, 1896.
    Captain, 16th November, 1898.
    Major, 9th March, 1901.
    Hon. Lieutenant in Army, 1st December, 1900.

Majors :

LOCKE, A. H., V.D. (*p.s.*), (*T.*) ... 27th January, 1903.
    Lieutenant, 16th February, 1884.
    Captain, 8th June, 1889.

Captains :

HARRIS, E. C. (*p.*)... ... ... 16th May, 1891.
    Second Lieutenant, 17th August, 1889.
DADE, H. (*p.s.*) ... ... 27th May, 1893.
    Second Lieutenant, 11th April, 1891.
    Lieutenant, 18th February, 1893.
MONSON, E. C. P. (*p.s.*) ... ... 12th February, 1896.
    Second Lieutenant, 17th December, 1892.
    Lieutenant, 25th November, 1893.
BRISCOE, T. F. H. (*p.s.*), (*H.*) ... 23rd February, 1898.
    Second Lieutenant, 26th May, 1894.
    Lieutenant, 21st February, 1895.
HOLLAND, H. W. (*p.*) ... ... 18th May, 1898.
    Second Lieutenant, 3rd February, 1894.
    Lieutenant, 20th November, 1895.
LYNCH, P. (*p.s.*) ... ... 18th January, 1899.
    Second Lieutenant, 14th August, 1895.
    Lieutenant, 29th July, 1896.
WARD, W. V. (*p.s.*) ... ... 18th April, 1900.
    Second Lieutenant, 17th April, 1895.
    Lieutenant, 19th February, 1896.
BARTHORPE, F. J., (*p.s.*) ... ... 12th December, 1900.
    Second Lieutenant, 8th January, 1896.
    Lieutenant, 26th May, 1897.
STEVENS, W., (*p.s.*) ... ... 3rd April, 1901.
    Second Lieutenant, 18th March, 1896.
    Lieutenant, 26th May, 1897.

BOTTERILL, G. P., (*p.s.*) ... ... 3rd April, 1901.
    Second Lieutenant, 17th February, 1897.
    Lieutenant, 6th July, 1898.

COHEN, I. (*p.s.*), (*H.*), (*S.*), (*I. of M.*) ... 23rd April, 1902.
    Second Lieutenant, 22nd February, 1899.
    Lieutenant, 25th July, 1900.

JACKSON, R. J. J., (*p.s.*) ... ... 27th January, 1903.
    Second Lieutenant, 5th July, 1899.
    Lieutenant, 19th June, 1901.

Lieutenants:

‡STEPHENSON, L. J., (*p.s.*) ... ... 25th July, 1900.
    Second Lieutenant, 15th July, 1899.
    Hon. Lieutenant in Army, 16th July, 1902.

WEIL, P. H., (*p.*) ... ... 19th June, 1901.
    Second Lieutenant, 22nd November, 1899.

HAMILTON, W. H., (*p.s.*) ... ... 19th June, 1901.
    Second Lieutenant, 10th January, 1900.

CARSON, S. M., (*p.*) ... ... 19th June, 1901.
    Second Lieutenant, 24th January, 1900.

THOMAS, C. E., (*p.s.*) ... ... 19th June, 1901.
    Second Lieutenant, 17th March, 1900.

ABBOTT, S. R., (*p.s.*) ... ... 30th November, 1901.
    Second Lieutenant, 27th June, 1900.

NORTH, P. M., (*p.s.*) ... ... 30th April, 1902.
    Second Lieutenant, 7th November, 1900.

JONES, R. E. (*p.s.*) ... . 30th April, 1902.
    Second Lieutenant, 28th November, 1900.

MOORE, E. S. (*p.s.*) ... ... 25th June, 1902.
    Second Lieutenant, 19th June, 1901.

FREETH, W. K. (*p.s.*) ... .. 27th January, 1903.
    Second Lieutenant, 16th November, 1901.

WILLIS, G. N. (*p.s.*) ... ... 27th January, 1903.
    Second Lieutenant, 19th March, 1902.

STILLWELL, E. H. (*p.s.*) ... ... 27th January, 1903.
    Second Lieutenant, 26th July, 1902.

Second Lieutenants:

PORTER, J. A.	...15th August, 1900.
GOODMAN, P. N. (*p.s.*)	...16th August, 1902.
LIMPENNY, S. W. J.	27th January, 1903.
DUNCAN-TEAPE, H. J. T.	10th February, 1903.
BURNETT, L. F.	... 3rd March, 1903.

Instructor of Musketry:

COHEN, I., Captain ... ... 26th April, 1902.

Adjutant:

PATTON-BETHUNE, D. E. B., Captain ... 1st April, 1899.
    Captain in Army, March 1, 1895.

Quarter-Master:

GARDINER, H. ... ... 21st April, 1903.

Medical Officers:

WATERHOUSE, W. D., Brigade-Surgeon Lieutenant-Colonel (*p*)
                                                    5th April, 1902.
    Acting Surgeon, 24th May, 1884.
    Surgeon-Captain, 20th July, 1889.

PRATT, J. D., M.D., Surgeon-Major (*p*)   2nd December, 1902.
    Acting Surgeon, 16th August, 1890.
    Surgeon-Captain, 11th April, 1891.

DUTCH, H., Surgeon-Captain (*p*) ... ... 15th July, 1896.
    Surgeon-Lieutenant, 20th May, 1893.

MARRETT, C. A., Surgeon-Captain (*p*) ... 11th June, 1902.
    Surgeon-Lieutenant, 17th May, 1899.

PARR, J. F. F., Surgeon-Lieutenant (*p*) 7th November, 1900.

Acting Chaplain:

SHEPPARD, Rev. E., D.D., C.V.O. ... ... 26th June, 1901.

SERGEANTS SERVING 7TH MAY, 1903.

PERMANENT STAFF SERGEANTS.

Regtl. No.			Date of Appointment.
5740	...	Sergeant-Major Dunkeld, G. ...	17th October, 1896
8696	...	Sergeant-Instructor Tomsett, E. S.	1st December, 1902
8435	...	,, ,, Williams, J. E.	1st May, 1901.

VOLUNTEER STAFF SERGEANTS.

Regtl. No.			Date of Appointment.
3906	...	Qr.-Mr.-Sgt. Warren, C. F. ...	21st February, 1901
3311	...	O.-R.-Qr.-Mr.-Sgt. Harrison, G. W.	1st January, 1900
4163	...	Staff-Armr. Sgt. Testi, G. C. .	14th April, 1903
5626	...	O.-R.-Qr.-Mr.-Sgt. Nathan, D. L.	6th May, 1903
6095	...	Band-Master Hopkins, J. ...	28th February, 1898
5939	...	Drum-Major Philip, G. T. ..	24th July, 1897
4926	...	Sgt.-Inst. Mky. Bryant, F. ...	9th March, 1903

COLOUR SERGEANTS.

Coy.	Regtl. No.	Rank.	Name.	Date of Appmt.
M	2354	Batt.-Sgt.-Maj.	Winkworth, C. T.	12th Dec., 1901
L	1835	Colour-Sergeant	Mathias, G.	14th Feb., 1891
J	2745	,,	Ansell, C. R. A.	19th Nov., 1892
G	3741	,,	Moore, G. F.	19th Nov., 1892
F	4337	,,	Rudman, F.	23rd Nov., 1897
M	4840	,,	Cullingworth, R. H.	17th Feb., 1898
A	5941	,,	Tew, Thos.	20th Dec., 1898
C	5068	,,	Hibberd, C. J.	1st Jan., 1900
E	4875	,,	Harrison, J.	6th Aug., 1898
B	6028	,,	Hodges, H. O.	26th Feb., 1901
H	5642	,,	Rush, Thos.	5th Nov., 1901
D	5177	,,	Galbraith, C. W.	1st Mar., 1903
K	5827	,,	McAdam, A.	9th Mar., 1903
D	7050	,,	Langdon, A. R.	6th May, 1903

SERGEANTS.

Coy.	Regtl. No.	Names.	Date of Appointment.
L	2794	Rampling, A. ...	31st January, 1891
M	2268	Ayres, G. W.	10th March, 1892
L	4878	Seal, W.	26th September, 1896
F	4626	Flude, B.	6th April, 1897
B	4432	French, S.	6th April, 1897
L	5197	Blatt, J.	23rd November, 1897
M	5583	Bath, F. W.	17th February, 1898
F	4822	Blacker, C. E.	17th February, 1898
E	4882	Shipway, F. W.	11th November, 1898
E	4116	Flude, C.	11th March, 1899
M	5337	Miller, H.	1st June, 1899
D	5619	Wakley, A.	11th November, 1899
L	5483	Greenshields, J.	11th November, 1899
H	3259	Richardson, W.	11th November, 1899
K	5883	Puttnam, A. W.	11th November, 1899
M	5684	Park, W.	14th November, 1899
J	3666	Jackson, G. H.	4th January, 1900
D	6264	Millard, A. W.	26th February, 1901
G	5027	Smith, W.	26th February, 1901
G	5315	Brooks, E. E.	12th March, 1901
E	4794	Walsh, T. W.	14th March, 1901
A	5446	Richards, R. G.	31st March, 1901
H	6124	Harris, M. P.	31st March, 1901
M	6013	Dumbleton, W.	31st March, 1901
K	6497	Drawbridge, W. H.	13th June, 1901
M	6339	Last, N.	23rd November, 1901
F	5847	Lewis, J.	1st February, 1902
J	6707	Rude, E.	1st February, 1902
K	5746	Child, F.	1st February, 1902
A	6638	Lawrie, H. A.	1st February, 1902
L	3223	Roberts, W. G.	1st February, 1902
C	6429	Hamilton, J.	25th March, 1902
A	6953	Horne, T. W.	30th October, 1902
B	5821	Smith, W. J.	30th October, 1902
B	6833	Salter, J.	30th October, 1902
H	6553	Hart, J.	30th October, 1902
L	6019	Bowers, W. G.	30th October, 1902

Armourer-Sergeant's Certificate.

Armourer-Sergeant Testi, G. C.

Sergeants in Possession of School of Instruction Certificate.

Quarter-Master Sergeant Warren, C. F.
Armourer-Sergeant Testi, G. C.
Company-Sergeant Major Shipway, F. W.
Colour-Sergeant Ansell, C. R. A.
,, Hibberd, Chas.
,, Cullingworth, R.
,, Hodges, H. O.
,, Tew, Thos.
Sergeant Bath, F. W.
,, Miller, H.

Sergeant in Possession of School of Cookery Certificate.

Sergeant Greenshields, J.

TOWER HAMLETS RIFLE VOLUNTEER BRIGADE.

Annual Returns, 1874 to 1891.

Year ending 31st October.	Efficients.	Non-efficient.	Total enrolled.	Proficients.		Present at Inspection.	Tactics.	Enrolled.	Struck off.
				Officers.	Sergeants.				
1874	647	191	838	73		625	—	*	*
1875	580	184	764	13	56	565	—	—	—
1876	637	82	719	13	55	618	—	—	—
1877	704	68	772	16	52	606	—	—	—
1878	746	73	819	18	50	680	—	—	—
1879	751	98	849	19	49	680	—	179	149
1880	884	19	903	21	50	788	—	315	261
1881	880	16	896	23	45	782	—	248	255
1882	837	32	869	23	47	760	4	134	161
1883	870	26	896	22	46	802	4	234	207
1884	937	34	971	25	47	857	5	313	238
1885	1048	27	1075	23	48	958	5	330	226
1886	1039	23	1062	21	46	987	5	248	261
1887	944	56	1000	23	47	945	9	269	331
1888	816	58	874	21	46	781	8	170	296
1889	807	56	863	19	43	785	7	295	306
1890	803	46	849	18	47	777	7	281	295
1891	826	43	869	18	49	764	7	176	156

* Statistics not available, 1874 to 1878.

Returns have been kept in more full detail since 1892.

TOWER HAMLETS RIFLE VOLUNTEER BRIGADE.

ANNUAL RETURNS, 1892 to 1896.

	1892	1893	1894	1895	1896
Efficients	826	838	858	858	877
Non-Efficients	48	29	20	34	36
P.C. of Efficients	94·50	96·65	97·70	96·18	96·05
Number of Officers	26	31	38	44	46
Officers Proficient	22	24	27	33	32
Sergeants Proficient	54	56	56	61	55
Tactics	8	7	8	7	7
Present at Inspection	743	760	804	805	882
Absent with Leave	108	95	77	86	97
Absent without Leave	25	11	8	10	9
Enrolled	170	170	131	149	194
Enlisted	19	19	17	15	11
Struck off	146	158	103	120	162
Joined Army for one year	—	—	—	—	—
BRIGADE CAMP—					
Officers	14	19	20	26	26
N.C. Officers and Men	308	307	311	330	332

TOWER HAMLETS RIFLE VOLUNTEER BRIGADE.

Annual Returns, 1897 to 1902.

	1897	1898	1899	1900	1901	1902
Efficients	896	921	950	1035	1010	847
Non-Efficients	21	16	11	11	16	68
P.C. of Efficients	97·70	98·29	98·85	98·94	98·41	94·21
Number of Officers	42	40	44	41	43	41
Officers Proficient	35	30	33	29	35	35
Sergeants Proficient	64	64	64	64	64	64
Tactics	6	5	4	5	4	4
Present at Inspection	854	893	894	966	914	779
Absent with Leave	98	51	68	101	59	90
Absent without Leave	12	Nil.	Nil.	3	6	35
Enrolled	210	225	277	315	208	147
Enlisted	30	16	31	35	21	13
Joined Army for one year	—	—	—	59	48	15
Struck off	176	189	222	195	207	245
Brigade Camp—						
Officers	25	26	23	25	27	28
N.C. Officers and Men	381	370	374	443	396	471

THE TOWER HAMLETS RIFLE VOLUNTEER BRIGADE.

LIST OF RETIRED OFFICERS.

1st JANUARY, 1874, to 7th MAY, 1903.

ABBOTT, B. R., Second Lieutenant, 4th February, 1893; resigned, 28th November, 1894.

ALDRIDGE, G., Second Lieutenant, 27th July, 1898; Lieutenant, 18th October, 1899; resigned, 5th March, 1902.

ALLEN, A. B. S., Sub-Lieutenant, 23rd June, 1875; resigned, 1st May, 1878.

ALSTON, A. W., Lieutenant, 16th February, 1884; Captain, 19th January, 1889; resigned, 28th January, 1891.

ANDERSON, G., Hon. Assistant Quarter-Master, 18th November, 1870; died, April, 1876.

ARMIT, J. L. E., late Lieutenant (h. p.), Royal Marines; Lieutenant, 30th July, 1879; resigned, December, 1882.

ASHTON, F., Sub-Lieutenant, 3rd May, 1876; resigned, 8th February, 1879.

BAILEY, E. E. E., Second Lieutenant, 1st January, 1898; Lieutenant, 25th January, 1899; resigned, 20th March, 1901.

BAPTIE, T. P., Second Lieutenant, 1st August, 1877; Lieutenant, 14th April, 1878; Captain, 5th November, 1879; resigned, February, 1885.

BARNETT, H. T., Second Lieutenant, 29th May, 1895; Lieutenant, 4th March, 1896; resigned, 16th November, 1898.

BATE, H. H., Second Lieutenant, 16th August, 1879; resigned, 12th January, 1881.

BENNETT, J., Sub-Lieutenant, 20th May, 1874; Captain, 16th May, 1877; resigned, March, 1889.

BENNETT, W. N., Ensign, 5th June, 1872; Lieutenant, 19th February, 1873; resigned, 29th May, 1874.

BIRDSEYE, J. K., from 5th Battalion Connaught Rangers; Lieutenant, 26th November, 1892; resigned, 20th October, 1898.

BOOT, F. G., Second Lieutenant, 8th May, 1878; Lieutenant, 22nd January, 1879; Captain, 5th November, 1879; resigned, 19th November, 1887.

BOVILL, H. J. M., Second Lieutenant, 10th November, 1880; Lieutenant, 2nd July, 1881; Captain, 6th March, 1886; resigned, 25th July, 1891.

BOWMAN, E., Second Lieutenant, 15th February, 1890; Lieutenant, 21st March, 1891; Captain, 11th April, 1891; resigned, 13th February, 1892.

BROWN, H., Ensign, 7th March, 1871; Lieutenant, 1st June, 1873; resigned, 23rd December, 1874.

BUCHANAN, M. G., Second Lieutenant, 9th July, 1892; resigned, 4th March, 1893.

BULL, T., Ensign, 14th May, 1868; Lieutenant, 24th November, 1870; Captain, 13th February, 1871; resigned, 12th February, 1876.

BULL, W., Ensign, 9th November, 1870; Lieutenant, 13th February, 1871; resigned, 12th February, 1876.

BURT, J. H., Second Lieutenant, 6th April, 1872; resigned, 12th October, 1878.

BUTLER, H. B., Second Lieutenant, 9th February, 1889; resigned, 27th June, 1891.

CALROW, E. F., Second Lieutenant, 7th February, 1879; Lieutenant, 1st July, 1881; Captain, 26th May, 1888; resigned, 6th July, 1889.

CHUBB, W. P. St. L., Sub-Lieutenant, 18th June, 1887; resigned, June, 1889.

CLARK, E., Second Lieutenant, 9th April, 1872; resigned, 28th June, 1876.

CLARKE, F., Second Lieutenant, 29th March, 1890; resigned, 6th February, 1892.

COAKLEY, J. L., Second Lieutenant, 7th October, 1896; Lieutenant, 25th January, 1899; Captain, 27th July, 1901; resigned, 11th January, 1903.

COHEN, G. E., Surgeon-Lieutenant, 4th March, 1899; to 1st Volunteer Battalion Duke of Cambridge's Own (Middlesex Regiment), 28th June, 1899.

COLEBROOK, G. E., Second Lieutenant, 7th March, 1900; Lieutenant, 19th June, 1901; died, 3rd February, 1903.

CONINGHAM, H., Second Lieutenant, 9th July, 1879; Lieutenant, 1st December, 1880; Captain, 4th October, 1884; Major, 20th November, 1895; Lieutenant-Colonel, 22nd January, 1898; Hon. Colonel, 26th July, 1899; resigned, 22nd December, 1900.

CONINGHAM, J. J., Second Lieutenant, 17th December, 1892; resigned, 7th July, 1894.

COTTEW, W. S., Second Lieutenant, 14th February, 1883; resigned, 17th December, 1883.

DAVIS, C., Lieutenant and Quarter-Master, 10th December, 1892; Honorary Captain, 16th December, 1892; resigned, 15th April, 1903.

DAVIS, F. A., Lieutenant, 25th January, 1882; resigned, 26th May, 1883.

DAVIS, H. E., Second Lieutenant, 19th April, 1891; Lieutenant, 9th April, 1892; Captain, 6th May, 1893; resigned, 4th December, 1895.

DE LA MARE, J., Lieutenant, 13th December, 1866; Captain, 18th November, 1870; Major and Hon. Lieutenant-Colonel, 27th November, 1889; resigned, 8th November, 1890.

DE METZ, A. A., Lieutenant, 25th September, 1860; Captain, 1st February, 1865; resigned, 21st March, 1877.

DOWSE, G. J., Second Lieutenant, 12th October, 1898; resigned, 7th March, 1900.

DUNCAN-TEAPE, N , Second Lieutenant, 28th November, 1900; died, 25th February, 1902.

EDMONDSON, R., Second Lieutenant, 7th March, 1900; resigned, 16th October, 1902.

ELKAN, A. E., Lieutenant, 3rd October, 1884; resigned, 8th December, 1888.

EMMET, C. A., Captain, 6th August, 1863; Major, 3rd April, 1871; resigned, 21st January, 1879.

EWER, J. E , Sub-Lieutenant, 14th July, 1875; Captain, 10th April, 1878; Major, 25th April, 1891; Hon. Lieutenant-Colonel, 20th January, 1894; resigned, 10th April, 1895.

EVANS-JACKSON, W. E., Second Lieutenant, 23rd June, 1894; Lieutenant, 20th November, 1895; resigned, 3rd March, 1897.

FARISH, A. F., Second Lieutenant, 27th February, 1891; Lieutenant, 19th September, 1891; Captain, 9th April, 1892; resigned, 18th May, 1898.

FARISH, R. V., Second Lieutenant, 22nd July, 1896; resigned, 16th November, 1898.

FERGUSON, G. G., Surgeon-Lieutenant, 7th February, 1891; to London Scottish, 28th March, 1894.

FERNEYHOUGH, C. T., Second Lieutenant, 7th March, 1871; Lieutenant 19th April, 1871; resigned, 23rd December, 1874.

FLETCHER, B., Lieutenant, 3rd January, 1867; Captain, 19th November 1867; Major, 26th February, 1881; Lieutenant-Colonel and Hon. Colonel, 20th December, 1890; resigned, 12th January, 1898.

FRENCH, J. H., Sub-Lieutenant, 11th October, 1876; resigned, 19th July, 1879.

GARRETT, J., Sub-Lieutenant, 31st January, 1877; resigned, 7th February, 1879.

GELLIBRAND, W. C., Lieutenant, 24th May, 1884; resigned, 19th November, 1887.

GOLE, J. R., Ensign, 19th April, 1871; Lieutenant, 1st June, 1873; resigned, 15th September, 1877.

GOLE, R., Lieutenant, 6th April, 1860; Captain, 21st February, 1868; Major, 18th January, 1889; resigned, June, 1889.

GRAY, T., Surgeon, 6th April, 1860; Surgeon Major, 1st July, 1881; resigned, 21st July, 1882.

GRICE, E., Second Lieutenant, 19th November, 1892; superseded for absence without leave, 12th December, 1894.

GUBBINS, E. G., Second Lieutenant, 30th May, 1900; resigned, 29th August, 1900.

HANDLEY, P. L., Lieutenant, 9th December, 1885 ; resigned, 13th July, 1889.
HAINES, A., Second Lieutenant, 18th October, 1879 ; Lieutenant, 1st December, 1880 ; resigned, 3rd October, 1883.
HEISER, H. G , Ensign, 2nd January, 1867 ; Lieutenant, 15th June, 1872 ; resigned, 12th February, 1876.
HERITAGE, F., Major, 23rd August, 1866 ; resigned, 12th January, 1881.
HEWITT, A., Lieutenant, 22nd March, 1884 ; resigned, July, 1887.
HEY, C. E. M., Surgeon-Lieutenant, 7th April, 1894 ; Second Lieutenant, 2nd November, 1894 ; resigned, 19th February, 1896.
HILL, W. N., Ensign, 31st December, 1870 ; Lieutenant, 16th March, 1871 ; Captain, 5th April, 1871 ; resigned, 3rd June, 1874.
HOLT, J., Captain, 6th April, 1860 ; Major, 30th December, 1867 ; Lieutenant-Colonel, 10th August, 1870 ; Command, 10th August, 1870 ; resigned, 28th June, 1876.
HOVELT, A. E. B., Second Lieutenant, 22nd March, 1899 ; Lieutenant, 25th July, 1900 ; to 5th Battalion King's Royal Rifle Corps, 3rd November, 1902.
HUMBERT, A., Second Lieutenant, 19th June, 1878 ; Lieutenant, 24th December, 1879 ; Captain, 18th November, 1881 ; resigned, 12th February, 1886.
HUMBERT, E., Second Lieutenant, 8th May, 1878 ; Lieutenant, 31st May, 1879 ; Captain, 4th May, 1881 ; resigned, 9th June, 1892.
HUNTER, L., Ensign, 6th January, 1871 ; Lieutenant, 19th April, 1871 ; Captain, 3rd May, 1871 ; resigned, 23rd December, 1874.
ISAACSON, C., Sub.-Lieutenant, 12th February, 1876 ; resigned, 21st May, 1879.
JACKSON, J. W., Assistant Surgeon, 10th April, 1886 ; Surgeon, 1st February, 1889 ; resigned, 6th July, 1889.
JONES, L. A., Second Lieutentant, 29th March, 1899 ; to 4th Battalion Royal Dublin Fusiliers, 22nd November, 1899.
LANE, C. W. G., Second Lieutenant, 10th July, 1895 ; resigned, 17th February, 1897.
LATHAM, C. W., Assistant Surgeon, 10th March, 1866 ; resigned, 21st March, 1877.
LAWSON, E. L., Hon. Assistant Quarter-Master, 29th May, 1865 ; Quarter-Master, 7th August, 1880 ; resigned, 29th July, 1882.
LAWSON, J. B., Second Lieutenant, 9th February, 1892 ; Lieutenant, 2nd July, 1892 ; resigned, 18th November, 1896.
LIVETT, J. J. W., from 1st Cambridge Rifle Volunteers ; Lieutenant, 14th June, 1884 ; Captain, 3rd August, 1889 ; resigned, 8th March, 1890.
MACKAY, A. R. H., Second Lieutenant, 6th November, 1895 ; Lieutenant, 26th May, 1897 ; resigned, 4th June, 1898.
MACKESON, E., Captain, 9th May, 1865 ; resigned, 18th March, 1874.
MAPLESON, A. F., Second Lieutenant, 19th June, 1878 ; **resigned**, December, 1881.

MAPLESON, J. H., Lieutenant-Colonel, 17th June, 1869; Hon. Colonel, August, 1881; Command, August, 1876; resigned, 2nd November, 1888.
MELLOR, W., Hon. Colonel, 20th February, 1867; died, June, 1886.
OPPENHEIM, J. H., Lieutenant, 19th November, 1867; Captain, 21st January, 1871; resigned, 18th March, 1874.
OWEN, J., Quarter-Master, 3rd December, 1870; resigned, 12th February, 1876.
PALMER, H., from 4th Manchester Rifle Volunteers; Captain, 14th December, 1889; to 3rd V.B. Essex, 11th March, 1893.
PARKINSON, J. H., Lieutenant, 14th March, 1867; Assistant Surgeon, 18th May, 1869; resigned, 11th November, 1874.
PARR, J. W. A., Lieutenant, 17th August, 1889; Captain, 15th March, 1890; Major, 9th February, 1898; resigned, 18th April, 1900.
PATON, M. C., Second Lieutenant, 6th January, 1894; Lieutenant, 21st July, 1894; Captain, 26th May, 1897; resigned, 20th July, 1901.
PAULL, J H., Surgeon, 25th September, 1860; Surgeon-Major, 1st July, 1881; resigned, 12th February, 1886.
PLATT, W. H., Surgeon, 6th January, 1871; to Volunteer Medical Staff Corps, 12th June, 1885.
POWNALL, E. P., Hon. Chaplain, 19th February, 1870; died, 10th February, 1900.
PRESTON, A. C., Second Lieutenant, 8th June, 1881; Lieutenant, 1st July, 1881; Captain, 6th March, 1886; Major, 18th April, 1900; resigned, with rank of Hon. Lieutenant-Colonel, 4th November, 1902.
PRESTON, S., Second Lieutenant, 22nd May, 1901; Lieutenant, 30th April, 1902; to 3rd East Yorks., 11th October, 1902.
PURSER, G., Ensign, 22nd December, 1869; Captain, 18th November, 1870; resigned, 22nd July, 1874.
RADLEY, W. L., Second Lieutenant, February, 1891; Lieutenant, 9th April, 1892; Captain, 20th November, 1895; resigned, 16th November, 1898.
RAPER, C., Ensign, 6th April, 1872; Lieutenant, 1st June, 1873; resigned, 23rd December, 1874.
REID, A. St. G. C., Second Lieutenant, 26th June, 1880; Lieutenant, 1st July, 1881; resigned, May, 1888.
ROBINSON, H. J., Sub.-Lieutenant, 21st February, 1877; resigned, November, 1877.
ROGERS, W., Hon. Chaplain, 25th September, 1860; died, January, 1896.
RONALDSON, C., Lieutenant, 26th April, 1865; Captain, 18th November, 1870; resigned, 19th November, 1879.
SCOTT, Second Lieutenant, 4th November, 1893; Lieutenant 12th December, 1894; Captain, 1st January, 1898; resigned, 4th January, 1899.

SEATON, E. M., Ensign, 7th March, 1871 ; Lieutenant, 14th June, 1871 ; Captain, 22nd September, 1875 ; resigned, 21st March, 1877.
SHELLEY, P. W. F., Lieutenant, 20th June, 1891 ; resigned, 3rd October, 1891.
SHIP, S. W., Second Lieutenant. 17th December, 1892 ; Lieutenant, 24th June, 1893 ; resigned, 17th June, 1896.
SHUTTLEWORTH, REV. H. C.. Acting Chaplain, 27th June, 1894 ; died, 24th October, 1900.
SILK, T., Lieutenant, 13th February, 1871 ; Captain, 5th June, 1872 ; resigned, 20th January, 1877.
SILVERLOCK, H. W., Second Lieutenant, 20th February, 1895 ; resigned, 10th March, 1897.
SIMPSON, J. P., Surgeon-Lieutenant, 16th December, 1893 ; Surgeon-Captain, 24th February, 1897 ; resigned, 31st January, 1900.
SLAUGHTER, E. J., Second Lieutenant, 13th May, 1896 ; Lieutenant, 22nd January, 1898 ; resigned, 7th March, 1900.
SLAUGHTER, R. J. A. T., Second Lieutenant, 13th May, 1896 ; Lieutenant, 22nd January, 1898 ; to 1st Volunteer Battalion East Kent Regiment, 17th May, 1898.
SMITH, T., Ensign, 7th March, 1871 ; Lieutenant, 1st June, 1873 ; Captain, 3rd February, 1875 ; Major and Hon. Lieutenant-Colonel, 15th November, 1890 ; resigned, 25th March, 1891.
SPENCER, H. T., Second Lieutenant, March, 1890 ; Lieutenant, 9th April, 1892 ; resigned, 14th January, 1893.
STANLEY, E. T. S., from 3rd Battalion Royal Irish Rifles ; Lieutenant, 18th April, 1894 ; resigned, 21st November, 1894.
STUART, C. C., Second Lieutenant, 9th February, 1898 ; Lieutenant, 25th January, 1899 ; to 3rd Prince of Wales's Volunteers (South Lancashire Regiment), 18th November, 1899.
TAYLOR, W., Captain, 29th June, 1861 ; resigned, 21st March, 1877.
THOMPSON, J. S., Lieutenant, 8th December, 1869 ; Captain, 4th April, 1877 ; Major and Hon. Lieutenant-Colonel, 3rd January, 1891 ; resigned, 1st December, 1897.
TIPPER, H. R., Lieutenant, 18th February, 1871 ; Captain, 5th June, 1872 ; resigned, 20th December, 1876.
TORKINGTON, J. K., Second Lieutenant, 15th May, 1895 ; Lieutenant, 4th March, 1896 ; resigned, 11th April, 1900.
TOWNSEND, E. G., Second Lieutenant, 6th February, 1892 ; resigned, 20th October, 1893.
TRAPP, F. H., Second Lieutenant, 22nd February, 1899 ; resigned, 25th July, 1900.
TULLY, T., Lieutenant, 14th March, 1877 ; Captain, 15th February, 1879 ; to 4th Volunteer Battalion East Surrey, 1st May, 1889.
TULLY, J. C., Sub-Lieutenant, 2nd June, 1877; Captain, 18th November, 1881 ; resigned, 14th June, 1884.
TUNSTALL, A. C., Surgeon-Lieutenant, 24th July, 1895 ; Surgeon-Captain, 17th August, 1898 ; to 4th London Brigade Bearer Company, 12th April, 1902.

WARD, F. G., Second Lieutenant, 14th May, 1902; resigned, 4th December, 1902.
WARD, J. B., Second Lieutenant, 6th July, 1889; Lieutenant, 19th October, 1889; Captain, 22nd November, 1900; to 3rd Volunteer Battalion Essex, 5th May, 1897.
WARREN, W. T., Second Lieutenant, 16th August, 1890; resigned, 6th February, 1892.
WATERFIELD, F., Second Lieutenant, 6th April, 1898; resigned, 24th January, 1900.
WATSON, W. G., Second Lieutenant, 28th March, 1900; services dispensed with, 7th September, 1901.
WARWICK, F. J. L., Surgeon-Lieutenant, 5th August, 1893; Surgeon-Captain, 16th December, 1896; to Volunteer Medical Staff Corps, 3rd February, 1899.
WETTENHALL, H. M., Second Lieutenant, 10th November, 1880; resigned, June, 1882.
WESTON, E. C., Second Lieutenant, 31st May, 1879; Lieutenant, 7th August, 1880; Captain, 21st July, 1882; resigned, July, 1887.
WHITE, O. M., Lieutenant, 16th August, 1881; resigned, 31st December, 1881; Acting Surgeon, 14th November, 1882; Surgeon, 13th February, 1886; Brigade Surgeon Lieutenant-Colonel, 14th December, 1889; died, 2nd March, 1898.
WHITEWAY, P., Second Lieutenant, 22nd February, 1899; resigned, 25th July, 1900.
WIGRAM, C., Captain, 6th April, 1860; Major, 4th December, 1867; Lieutenant-Colonel, 28th June, 1876; Hon. Lieutenant-Colonel, 7th April, 1885; Command, November, 1888; resigned, 22nd November, 1890.
WILDE, E. T. R., Ensign, 5th June, 1861; Lieutenant, 21st November, 1862; Captain, 1st January, 1866; Major, 21st May, 1879; Lieutenant-Colonel and Hon. Colonel, 15th December, 1888; Command, 23rd November, 1890; resigned, 24th January, 1903.
WILLIAMS, C. W., Lieutenant, 2nd August, 1876; Captain, 7th February, 1879; resigned, 1st May, 1880.
WILLIAMS, L. S., Second Lieutenant, 15th July, 1893; Lieutenant, 21st July, 1894; Captain, 18th November, 1896; resigned, 3rd April, 1901.
WILLOUGHBY, L. B., from 3rd Middlesex Rifle Volunteers; Lieutenant, 12th February, 1887; to 3rd London, 21st December, 1889.
WILSON, H., Second Lieutenant, 30th January, 1895; resigned, 28th October, 1896.
WOODS, J. F., Surgeon-Lieutenant, 29th July, 1896; resigned, 28th July, 1897.
WRIGHT, H., Lieutenant, 25th January, 1882; Captain, 26th May, 1888; Hon. Major, 12th February, 1896; resigned, 12th December, 1900.

TOWER HAMLETS RIFLE VOLUNTEER BRIGADE.

FORMER ADJUTANTS.

Lowry, A., Captain, May, 1860; resigned, June, 1880.
Burge, B. H., Captain, December, 1872; to 1st Lanark Volunteer Rifles, 1st January, 1876.
Barnett, E. de B., Captain, 4th King's Own Regiment, June, 1880; resigned, October, 1881.
Schrieber, F. B., Captain, late 1st Foot, from 1st Cambridge Rifle Volunteers, 1st October, 1881; resigned, February, 1882.
Richardson, E. R. S., Captain, Prince of Wales' North Staffordshire Regiment, February, 1882; resigned, April, 1884.
Maude, R. J., Captain, Rifle Brigade, 1st April, 1884; period of service expired, 1st April, 1889.
Money, C. G. C., Captain, Northumberland Fusiliers, 1st April, 1889; period of service expired, 1st April, 1894.
Coddington, H. A., Captain, Royal Irish Fusiliers, 2nd April, 1894; period of service expired, 1st April, 1899.

FORMER SERGEANT-MAJORS.

Tustin, W. H., from 50th Regiment, July, 1860; discharged, March, 1877.
Woodham, J., from 59th Regiment, February, 1862; discharged, August, 1882.
Vance, T. E., from 8th King's, 1st May, 1877; discharged, May, 1890.
Monk, C., from Royal Marine Artillery, joined 28th July, 1899; Sergeant-Major, May, 1890; discharged, 30th September, 1896.

APPENDIX.

RECORD OF EVENTS

FROM 1ST JANUARY, 1874. TO 7TH MAY, 1903.

1874.

January 1st—Authority for Amalgamation of 6th Tower Hamlets Rifle Volunteer Corps with the 1st. Headquarters at 112, Shaftesbury Street, New North Road.
January 10th—First Parade of Amalgamated Corps.
March 30th—Supper of Sergeants at Headquarters to celebrate the amalgamation.
April 6th, Easter Monday—Field Day at Putney.
June 13th—Brigade Drill in Regent's Park; present 625.
July 4th—Annual Inspection in Regent's Park; about 650 present.
July 18th—Review at Wimbledon.
August—Establishment reduced from 16 to 12 Companies,
October 25th—Church Parade at St. Paul's Cathedral.
November—Scarlet Uniforms with blue facings approved.
December 12th—Companies re-arranged for the reduction of the establishment.

Battalion Drills were held at Headquarters in Uniform nearly every Saturday, and at Ilford and Hackney Downs. Ranges were at Ilford and Loughton.

New Forage Caps were issued to the Members of the 6th, and the trousers had a red stripe put on them. A Company was told off for duty each week to mount guard during drill, the Officer on duty had to make a report.

1875.

February 11th—Prize Distribution at Headquarters, by Mr. John Holmes, M.P.
June 12th—Brigade Drill in Regent's Park.

June 30th—Guard of Honour, in grey uniform, for Duke of Westminster laying the Foundation Stone of the East London Hospital for Childen.
July 24th—Review at Wimbledon. Regiment went by boat to Putney.
August 7th—Annual Inspection in Regent's Park ; present 565.
October 31st—Church Parade at St. Paul's Cathedral.
December 22nd—Prize Distribution at Headquarters, by the Lord Mayor, W. J. Richmond Cotton, Esq.

Out-door Battalion Drills were at Hampstead Heath and Ilford ; in both places blank was fired.
Range at Ilford ; the range at Loughton was given up in April.
Extensive repairs and some alterations were made at Headquarters.
The orders were signed by the two Adjutants, Captains Lowry and Burge.
There was a School of Arms at Headquarters.

1876.

April 15th—A Detachment of 5 Officers, 40 Non-Commissioned Officers and Men, and 23 Drums and Fifes marched to Watford. (Each man paid his own expenses.)
April 16th—Church Parade with Watford Company of 2nd Herts. R.V.C., and March continued to Berkhampstead.
April 17th, Easter Monday—Field Day at Tring.
April 22nd—Military Funeral of Quarter-Master George Anderson.
June 3rd—Brigade Drill in Regent's Park.
June 13th—Colonel Holt's last parade as Commanding Officer.
June 21st—Farewell Dinner by Officers at Café Royal to Colonel Holt.
July 1st—Review by Prince of Wales in Hyde Park. Annual Inspection after Review ; present 618.
August—Colonel J. H. Mapleson assumed command on the retirement of Colonel John Holt.
October 29th—Church Parade at St. Paul's Cathedral.
December 5th—Guard of Honour, in scarlet, for Lord Mayor, Sir Thomas White, opening a Bazaar in Poplar.
December 20th—Prize Distribution at Headquarters by General Lord Alfred Paget.

Captain Lowry signed the Orders after 27th January, Captain Burge having been transferred to Glasgow.
Commanding Officer's Parades in Uniform at Headquarters on Saturdays with frequent March Outs.
Out-Door Parades at Hampstead Heath and Ilford.
The appointment of a Company for weekly duty was discontinued, and Company Drills were fixed for Tuesdays and Thursdays. There were three Companies drilling each night, so that the Half-Battalions drilled alternate weeks under the Major of the Half-Battalion.

New Musketry Regulations came in force on 1st November.

New Rules for enrolment of Recruits were made : "After the 1st October, Recruits will be required to pay : On Enrolment, 5s.; on receiving a Rifle, 2s. 6d.; and on obtaining an Order for Uniform, 2s. 6d.; which amount they will be credited with when they receive their Uniform."

1877.

March 17th—March of Guards and Volunteers, under Lord Abinger, through the West End.
March 31st—A Detachment, consisting of 5 Officers and 60 Non-Commissioned Officers and Men, marched to St. Albans. (Each man paid his own expenses.)
April 1st—Church Parade at St. Albans Abbey, and march to Luton.
April 2nd, Easter Monday—Field Day at Dunstable.
May 2nd—A Guard of Honour for Duchess of Teck opening East London Hospital.
June 9th—March to Wimbledon and Field Day there with Scots Guards.
June 30th—Annual Inspection in Regent's Park ; present 606.
August 11th to 18th—A Detachment at Aldershot.
August 25th—Fête at Alexandra Palace in aid of the Prize Fund.
October 28th—Church Parade at St. Paul's Cathedral.
December 17th—Prize Distribution at Headquarters by Lady Abinger.

Company Drills were in plain clothes.
Commanding Officer's Uniform Parades at Headquarters on Saturdays, and at Ilford and Hackney Downs.
Range at Ilford.

1878.

April 20th—A Detachment of 7 Officers, 64 Non-Commissioned Officers and Men, 3 Buglers, and 16 Drums and Fifes, marched to Watford, being met on arrival by local Company of 2nd Herts. Volunteer Rifle Corps. (Each man paid his own expenses.)
April 21st—Church Parade, and march to St. Albans ; band of local Company playing us in.
April 22nd, Easter Monday—Back to Headquarters by Route March.
June 1st—Brigade Drill in Hyde Park.
June 10th, Whit-Monday—A Detachment marched to Waltham Abbey, returning by train.
June 29th—Annual Inspection in Regent's Park ; present 680.
July 27th to August 3rd—A Detachment of 5 Officers and 86 Non-Commissioned Officers and Men to Aldershot, Guard's Ground, North Camp, forming part of the 3rd Provisional Battalion Rifle Volunteers.

October 27th—Church Parade at St. Paul's Cathedral.
December 16th—Prize Distribution at Headquarters by Colonel Gipps.

In April, a War Office Order was issued, "Officers will wear cross belts and pouches in full dress and undress."

Officers were requested in May to supply themselves with the new pattern helmets.

A Regimental Ambulance Class was formed in September.

Uniform Parades at Headquarters on Saturdays, and Out-door Drills on Hackney Downs and at Ilford.

The Range was at Ilford.

1879.

March 8th—Military Funeral of Drum-Major Taylor.
May 31st—Brigade Drill in Hyde Park; present 321.
June 28th—Annual Inspection in Regent's Park; present 680.
July 5th to 12th—A Detachment at Aldershot, Rushmore Hill, forming part of 5th Provisional Battalion Rifle Volunteers.
October 19th—Church Parade at St. Paul's Cathedral.
December 17th—Prize Distribution at Headquarters by Colonel Samuda, M.P.

In January, helmets were issued.

In February, it was ordered, "Cross belts will be no longer worn by Officers in undress."

Officers' undress was altered from the frock coat to patrol jacket.

An attempt to raise a Marching Column for Waltham Abbey, &c., at Easter was not successful.

Assistant Sergeant-Instructors were appointed from the Sergeants by competition.

Uniform Parades were at Headquarters on Saturdays, with frequent marches out.

Battalion Drills in Regent's Park, Hackney Downs and Wanstead Flats.

Range at Ilford.

Tent pitching for the Aldershot Detachment was practiced on Hackney Downs.

1880.

March 29th, Easter Monday—Field Day at Brighton; present 380.
May 8th—Brigade Drill in Hyde Park; present 514.
June 26th—Annual Inspection in Regent's Park; present 788.
August 7th to 14th—A Detachment of 3 Officers, 6 Sergeants and 102 Rank and File to Aldershot to join Provisional Battalion Rifle Volunteers.

October 24th—Church Parade at St. Paul's Cathedral.
December 6th—Prize Distribution at Shoreditch Town Hall by Mr. Ritchie, M.P.

Field Officers were ordered to have gilt sword scabbards, hilts, and spurs. Other Officers, gilt hilts and gold sword-knots for full dress, in accordance with the regulations for regiments clothed in scarlet.

Black rifle slings were exchanged for white ones.

Drill at Headquarters as usual, with Out-door Parades on Hampstead Heath, at Ilford, and in Regent's Park; blank being fired.

The Range was at Ilford.

1881.

April 18th, Easter Monday—Field Day at Brighton; present 418.
May 28th—Brigade Drill in Hyde Park; present 458.
June 25th—Annual Inspection in Hyde Park; present 782.
July 9th—Review by H.M. The Queen at Windsor.
August 6th to 13th—A Detachment of 5 Officers, 93 Non-Commissioned Officers and Men to Aldershot to join the 1st Provisional Battalion Volunteer Brigade encamped on Rushmore.
October 23rd—Church Parade at St. Paul's Cathedral.
December 12th—Prize Distribution at Shoreditch Town Hall by Miss Wilde.

Battalion Drills were held in Regent's Park and at Headquarters.
Range at Ilford.

In April, Officers were ordered to provide themselves with the new shoulder straps and badges of rank.

The Officers' Mess was established; the first of the Quarterly Dinners was held at the "Albion," Covent Garden, the others at the "Horse Shoe."

1882.

April 3rd, Easter Monday—Field Day at Portsmouth; present 452.
May 20th—Brigade Drill in Hyde Park; present 484.
June 24th—Annual Inspection in Hyde Park; present 760.
October 22nd—Church Parade at St. Paul's Cathedral.
December 21st—Prize Distribution at Headquarters by Lady Jane Taylor (wife of General Sir R. Taylor).

The Officers' Mess was held at the "Horse Shoe."
Battalion Drills took place at Headquarters on Saturdays in uniform, with Parades in Regent's Park.
Range at Ilford.

A Detachment was not sent to the Provisional Battalion at Aldershot this year.

In March, the ribbons of the Glengarries were ordered to be eight inches in length.

1883.

March 26th, Easter Monday—Field Day at Brighton; present 401.
April 4th—Outpost work at Hampstead Heath.
May 26th—Brigade Drill in Hyde Park; present 428.
June 30th—Annual Inspection in Hyde Park; present 802.
August 11th to 18th—Aldershot, Rushmore (present 131); forming part of the 2nd Provisional Battalion Rifle Volunteers.
October 21st—Church Parade at St. Paul's Cathedral.
December 17th—Prize Distribution at Headquarters by Colonel Samuda.

Drills were frequently held in Regent's Park, the Battalion going by rail to Camden Town and marching thence.

The Officers held their Mess quarterly at the " Horse Shoe."

1884.

March 26th—Regimental Smoker at Headquarters.
April 14th, Easter Monday—Field Day at Dover; present 468.
May 17th—Brigade Drill at Wimbledon; present 461.
July 5th—Annual Inspection in Hyde Park; present 857.
July 11th—Guard of Honour for Prince of Wales opening the Bethnal Green Museum.
August 9th to 16th—A Detachment at Aldershot with Provisional Battalion Rifle Volunteers.
October 26th—Church Parade at St. John's, Hoxton.
December 8th—Prize Distribution by Lord Mayor, G. S. Nottage, Esq., at Shoreditch Town Hall.

Battalion Drills were held at the Tower, Ilford and Regent's Park, and at Headquarters on Saturdays.

Range at Ilford.

Officers still held their Mess at the " Horse Shoe."

Leggings of regulation pattern were issued.

1885.

April 6th, Easter Monday—Field Day at Brighton; present 487. The Battalion found Signallers for the Marching Column.
May 30th—Brigade Drill in Regent's Park; present 567.
July 4th—Annual Inspection in Hyde Park; present 958.

August 8th to 15th—Detachment at Aldershot with the Provisional Battalion Rifle Volunteers.
October 25th—Church Parade at St. Paul's Cathedral.
December 7th—Prize Distribution by Lord Mayor, Sir John Staples, at Shoreditch Town Hall.

In May the Standard for Recruits was raised to 5 ft. 5 in. with 34 in. chest measurement.
The Snider's were called in to be exchanged for Martini Henry's.
The Officers continued to hold their Mess at the "Horse Shoe."
Battalion Drills were held at the Tower and Regent's Park, besides Headquarters.
Ranges were at Wormwood Scrubbs and Roxeth Harrow.

1886.

March 8th—Guard of Honour for Lord Mayor, Sir John Staples, at Town Hall, Poplar.
April 23rd, Easter—Detachment and 2 Gardner Machine Guns with Marching Column to Canterbury and Dover.
April 26th, Easter Monday—Field Day at Dover; present 522.
May 22nd—Brigade Drill in Regent's Park; present 559.
June 26th—Annual Inspection in Hyde Park; present 987.
August 7th to 14th—Detachment of 175 and 2 Gardner Machine Guns to Aldershot, Church Plateau, North Camp, forming part of the 5th Provisional Battalion Rifle Volunteers.
October 17th—Church Parade at St. Paul's Cathedral.
December 6th—Prize Distribution at Cowper Street School, City Road, by Mrs. Banister Fletcher; Colonel Moncrieff, who had just been appointed Honorary Colonel, being prevented attending.

Officers' Mess at the "Horse Shoe" in February, May, July, and November.

1887.

April 8th—Marching Column, 86 all told and four Gardner Machine Guns, to Canterbury.
April 9th—On to Dover.
April 11th, Easter Monday—Field Day at Dover; present 467.
May 14th—Parade for lining part of Whitechapel on occasion of H.M. the Queen opening the People's Palace, Mile End.
May 21st—Brigade Drill in Regent's Park; present 430.
June 25th—Annual Inspection in Hyde Park; present 945.
July 2nd—March Past before H.M. the Queen at Buckingham Palace; present 416.
July 9th—Jubilee Review by H.M. the Queen at Aldershot, the Hon. Colonel, General Moncrieff, leading the Battalion past.

August 6th to 13th—A Detachment at Aldershot, with 1st Provisional Battalion Rifle Volunteers.
October 16th—Church Parade at St. John's, Hoxton.
December 17th—Prize Distribution at Shoreditch Town Hall, by Colonel Holt.

Battalion Drills were held at Headquarters on Saturdays, in uniform, and at the Tower, Wanstead Flats, Regent's Park, &c.
Ranges at Wormwood Scrubbs and Roxeth Harrow.
Officers' Mess at the " Horse Shoe."

1888.

March 30th—Marching Column, with the Gardner Machine Guns, to Ashford.
March 31st—On to Dover.
April 2nd, Easter Monday—Field Day at Dover; present 415.
April 28th—A Regimental Concert was held at Shoreditch Town Hall.
May 26th—Brigade Drill in Regent's Park; present 521.
July 7th—Annual Inspection in Hyde Park; present 781.
August 11th to 18th—A Detachment of 150, with Gardner Machine Guns, at Aldershot, Rushmore Hill.
October 28th—Church Parade at St. Paul's Cathedral.
November—Colonel Clifford Wigram assumed command on retirement of Colonel J. H. Mapleson.
December 8th—Prize Distribution by Colonel Stracey at Shoreditch Town Hall.

Officers were ordered to wear white gloves.
Orders were issued that in future the pouch was not to be worn by Sergeants on the waist-belt.
Battalion Drills were held at Chingford and Wormwood Scrubbs, besides Headquarters.
Ranges were at Wormwood Scrubbs, and at Roxeth Harrow.
Officers' Mess at the " Horse Shoe."
Battalion transferred to Grenadier Guards' Brigade.

1889.

May 25th—Brigade Drill in Regent's Park; present 194.
June 29th—Annual Inspection in Hyde Park; present 785.
August 3rd to 8th—A Detachment at Aldershot to form with 3rd London, the 2nd Provisionial Battalion Rifle Volunteers.
August 7th—Review before H.I.M. the Emperor of Germany; a further Detachment to complete Battalion, coming down for the day, making 314 present.
October 12th—Church Parade at St. Nicholas Cole Abbey, Queen Victoria Street.

December 3rd—Smoking Concert at Prince's Hall.
December 16th—Prize Distribution at Headquarters, by Lord Harris, Under Secretary of State for War, and Governor Designate of Bombay.

A Route March and Field Day for Easter Monday, 22nd April was proposed, but countermanded.

Outdoor Drills were held at Wormwood Scrubbs, Chingford and Hampstead Heath.

Ranges at Wormwood Scrubbs and Roxeth Harrow.

The Duty Roster for Officers was started.

In April, Officers were ordered to provide themselves with regulation pattern brown gloves for undress.

Officers' Mess at the "Horse Shoe."

In March this year "M" Company was allotted to the Machine Gun Battery and the Bearers.

A Morris Tube Club was started at Headquarters.

1890.

April 7th, Easter Monday—Machine Gun Battery with Colonel Stracey's Brigade at Dover. Illustrations in "Illustrated London News" and "Daily Graphic," of 12th April, 1890.
May 31st—Brigade Drill at Chingford.
June 26th—Guard of Honour, at Limehouse, for H.R.H. Princess Christian.
June 28th—Annual Inspection in Hyde Park; present 777.
October 19th—Church Parade at St. John's, Hoxton.
November 23rd—Colonel E. T. Rodney Wilde assumed command on retirement of Colonel Clifford Wigram.
December 15th—Prize Distribution at Headquarters by Colonel Wigram, who had resigned 22nd November, 1890.

The Battalion did not go to Aldershot for Camp, but the Ambulance Detachment, under Surgeon White, attended there from 2nd to 9th August.

New equipment was issued in September.

Battalion Drills were at Enfield, Chingford, Wormwood Scrubbs.

Ranges at Wormwood Scrubbs and Roxeth Harrow.

The Officers moved their Mess to the "Inns of Court" Hotel, and later to Café Royal.

The Sergeants' Mess held Debates on military subjects.

1891.

March 7th—A Military Tournament was held at Headquarters.
March 14th—Sergeants' Mess Annual Dinner at Headquarters.
March 30th, Easter Monday—Brigade Field Day at Shorncliffe.

May 21st—Officers' Dance at Rooms of Royal Society of British Artists, Suffolk Street, Pall Mall.
May 30th—Brigade Drill at Chingford; present 318.
July 11th—Review at Wimbledon before H.I.M. Emperor of Germany.
July 11th—Annual Inspection after the Review; present 764.
July 19th—Church Parade at St. Botolph's, Bishopsgate.
August 1st to 8th—Brigade Camp Aldershot, Farnborough Common; 243 all told, and four Gardner Machine Guns.
December 14th—Prize Distribution at Headquarters by Mrs. Wilde.

In January a new pattern Fatigue Cap for Officers was approved, and a regimental pattern swagger cane was adopted.

The New Equipment was continued to be issued.

Battalion Drills were at the Tower, Wormwood Scrubbs, Chingford, and Dalston Barracks.

Ranges at Wormwood Scrubbs, Roxeth Harrow, and Ilford.

Officers' Mess was held at Café Royal.

1892.

March 5th—Sergeants' Mess Annual Dinner at Headquarters.
March 19th—Military Tournament at Headquarters.
April 14th to 18th, Eastertide—Machine Gun Battery at Chatham. Illustrations in "Daily Graphic," 20th April, 1892.
May 2nd—History of Tower Hamlets Rifle Volunteer Brigade, by Colonel Wilde, published by Messrs. Coningham Bros.
May 3rd—Officers' Dance at the Rooms of the Royal Society of British Artists, Suffolk Street, Pall Mall.
May 28th—Brigade Tactical Field Day at Chingford.
July 9th—Annual Inspection in Hyde Park; present 743.
July 17th—Church Parade at St. Botolph's, Bishopsgate.
July 30th to August 6th—Brigade Camp, Aldershot, Bourley Road; 14 Officers, 308 Non-Commissioned Officers and Men.
October 22nd—Field Day, Wimbledon; Machine Gun Battery only.
December 19th—Prize Distribution at Headquarters by Colonel Trotter, commanding East London Volunteer Brigade.

Battalion Drills at the Tower, and Chingford.

Ranges at Wormwood Scrubbs, and Ilford.

Officers' Mess held at Café Royal.

Sergeant-Instructor J. H. Wise died on 30th April; the funeral was private, by request.

1893.

March 11th—Military Tournament at Headquarters.
March 30th to April 3rd, Eastertide — Machine Gun Battery at Chatham. Illustrations in "Daily Graphic," 5th April, 1893.

May 2nd—Officers' Dance at Westminster Town Hall.
May 13th,—Machine Guns at Victoria and St. George's Tournament.
May 27th—Brigade Field Day at Chingford.
June 1st - A Challenge Cup for Ambulance Work, presented by the Ladies of the Officers.
July 1st—Annual Inspection in Hyde Park ; present 760.
July 6th —Detachment to form Guard of Honour on Marriage of Duke and Duchess of York.
July 16th—Church Parade at St. Botolph's, Bishopsgate.
August 5th to 12th—Brigade Camp, Aldershot, Rushmoor Green ; 19 Officers, 307 Non-Commissioned Officers and Men.
October 28th—Brigade Field Day at Wimbledon.
December 18th — Prize Distribution at Headquarters by Lord Methuen, C.B., C.M.G.

Battalion Drills were held at Chingford and Ilford.
Ranges at Wormwood Scrubbs and Ilford.
Officers' Mess at Café Royal.

1894.

March 10th—Military Tournament at Headquarters.
March 22nd to 26th, Eastertide—Machine Gun Battery at Winchester.
March 31st—Sergeants' Mess Annual Dinner at "Falstaff" Restaurant.
April 4th—Officers' Dance at Rooms of Royal Society of British Artists, Suffolk Street, Pall Mall.
April 14th—Regimental Smoking Concert at Headquarters.
April 28th—Outpost work at Ealing.
May 14th, Whit Monday—Field Firing at Pirbright.
May 26th—Brigade Field Day in Epping Forest.
June 19th—Inspection of Officers at Headquarters by Brigadier.
June 30th—Detachment at Opening of Tower Bridge by Prince of Wales.
June 30th – Annual Inspection in Hyde Park ; present 804.
July 8th—Church Parade, St. Nicholas Cole Abbey, Queen Victoria Street.
August 4th to 11th—Brigade Camp, Aldershot, Rushmore Hill, 20 Officers, 311 Non-Commissioned Officers and Men. A Detachment went by Route March.
December 10th—Prize Distribution at Headquarters by Colonel Oliphant.

A Cyclist Section was formed in August.
Battalion Drills were at Chingford and Ilford.
Ranges at Wormwood Scrubbs and Ilford.
New pattern Field Service Cap in lieu of the Glengarries was issued in July.

Officers held their Mess at the Café Royal.

In September, the Quarter-Master, Lieutenant Davis, and a few friends presented a handsome Challenge Cup, to be competed for on conditions similar to those of the " Daily Telegraph " Cup.

1895.

February 2nd—Concentration March with Brigade of Guards and Volunteer Battalions of the Home District.
March 16th—Sergeants' Mess Annual Dinner at "Falstaff" Restaurant.
May 13th—Sergeants' Mess re-opened at Headquarters after the alterations.
May 18th—Brigade Tactical Field Day at Aldershot.
June 3rd, Whit Monday—Field Firing at Pirbright.
June 13th—Guard of Honour for H.R.H. Duchess of Albany opening a Flower show at Shoreditch.
June 16th—Church Parade at St. Nicholas Cole Abbey, Queen Victoria Street.
June 22nd—Military Tournament on re-opening the Headquarters after extensive alterations and repairs. Bust of Colonel Wilde unveiled in the Officers' Ante-room by General Moncrieff.
June 25th—Inspection of Officers by the Brigadier at Headquarters.
June 29th—Annual Inspection in Hyde Park; present 805.
August 3rd to 10th—Brigade Camp, Aldershot, Rushmoor, 26 Officers, 330 Non-Commissioned Officers and Men.
September 28th—Military Funeral of Colour-Sergeant Bignell.
October 26th—Brigade Time Night March with Guards.
December 9th—Prize Distribution by Mrs. Moncrieff at Headquarters.

Telegraphic Address "Towerlike, London," was registered in August.

Battalion Drills were at Chingford and Ilford.

Ranges at Wormwood Scrubbs and Ilford.

Extensive additions and alterations were made at Headquarters including new Dressing Room, &c., for Officers, with lockers, and greatly improved Ante-room.

Officers' Mess at Café Royal.

1896.

February 10th—Officers' Dance, Westminster Town Hall.
May 15th—Outfit allowance for Subaltern Officers granted by the War Office.
May 16th—Brigade Tactical Field Day at Pirbright.
May 25th, Whit Monday—Field Firing at Pirbright.
June 14th—Church Parade, St. Nicholas Cole Abbey.
July 4th—Annual Inspection in Hyde Park; present 882.

August 1st to 8th—Brigade Camp, Aldershot, Bourley Road ; 26 Officers, 332 Non-Commissioned Officers and Men.
October 7th—Sergeant-Major G. Dunkeld appointed.
November 7th—Sergeants' Mess Annual Dinner at Headquarters.
December 7th—Prize Distribution at Headquarters, by General Sir Francis W. Grenfell, G.C.M.G., K.C.B.

Battalion Drills were at Ilford, Hackney Downs, and Woolwich Common.
Firing at Wormwood Scrubbs and Ilford.
The Officers held their Mess at Café Royal.

1897.

April 10th—Military Tournament at Headquarters.
May 3rd – Officers' Dance at Westminster Town Hall.
June 7th, Whit Monday—Field Firing at Pirbright.
June 20th—Church Parade at St. Nicholas Cole Abbey, Queen Victoria Street.
June 22nd — Detachment for Diamond Jubilee ; Brigade Bearer Company paraded.
July 3rd—Annual Inspection in Hyde Park ; present 854.
July 12th—Guard of Honour furnished.
July 31st to August 7th—Brigade Camp, Aldershot, Danger Hill ; 25 Officers, 381 Non-Commissioned Officers and Men.
December 13th—Prize Distribution at Headquarters by General Trotter.

New pattern frogs were issued in January.
A new pattern Officers' Mess jacket and waistcoat was sealed as approved.
Out-door Parades at Chingford, Victoria Park, and Woolwich.
Ranges at Ilford, Wormwood Scrubbs, and Bisley.
Officers held their Quarterly Mess at Café Royal.

1898.

January 22nd—Night March of Volunteers of the Home District ; present 387.
February 9th—Guard of Honour for H.R.H. the Duchess of Fife, opening New Wing of Hackney Town Hall.
March 19th—Military Tournament at Headquarters.
April 25th—Sergeants' Mess, Annual Dinner at Headquarters.
May 12th – Officers' Mess (Ladies' Dinner) at Café Royal.
May 30th, Whit Monday—Field Firing, Pirbright.
June 12th—Church Parade, St. Nicholas Cole Abbey, Queen Victoria Street.

June 21st—Inspection of Officers at Headquarters by Brigadier.
July 2nd—Annual Inspection, Hyde Park; present 893.
July 30th to August 5th—Brigade Camp, Aldershot, Bourley; 26 Officers, 370 Non-Commissioned Officers and Men.
December 12th – Prize Distribution at Headquarters, by Colonel Oliphant.

Out-door Parades were at Chingford, Victoria Park, and Hackney Marshes.
Ranges at Wormwood Scrubbs, Ilford and Pirbright.
In November the Officers met to consider proposed further addition at Headquarters.
Officers' Mess still met Quarterly at the Café Royal.

1899.

March 25th—Military Tournament at Headquarters.
April 15th—Sergeants' Mess Annual Dinner at Headquarters.
May 16th—Officers' Mess (Ladies' Dinner) at Café Royal.
May 22nd, Whit Monday—Field Firing at Pirbright.
June 6th—Inspection of Officers at Headquarters by Brigadier.
June 11th—Church Parade at St. Nicholas Cole Abbey, Queen Victoria Street.
July 1st—Annual Inspection in Hyde Park; present 894.
July 8th—Review by Prince of Wales on Horse Guards' Parade.
August 5th to 12th—Brigade Camp at Aldershot, Cove; 23 Officers and 374 Non-Commissioned Officers and Men.
December 11th — Prize Distribution at Headquarters by Colonel Ricardo.

Out-door Parades were at Chingford and Victoria Park.
Ranges at Wormwood Scrubbs and Pirbright.
A Cyclist Company was started.
Officers' Mess at Café Royal.

1900.

January 18th—" Send off " of City Imperial Volunteers.
March 21st—Guard of Honour for Princess Christian opening the Hackney Baths.
March 31st—Military Tournament at Headquarters.
May 14th—Sergeants' Mess Annual Dinner at Manchester Hotel, Aldersgate Street.
May 21st—Officers' Mess (Ladies' Dinner) at Hotel Cecil.
June 4th, Whit-Monday—Field Firing at Pirbright.

July 7th— Annual Inspection at the Tower; present 966.
August 4th to 11th— Mobilization of Thames Valley Defence Force, T.H.R.V.B. in camp at Chatham; 25 Officers, 442 Non-Commissioned Officers and Men.
October 29th—Return of City Imperial Volunteers.
November 3rd—Dinner to City Imperial Volunteers, and reception afterwards at Headquarters. Illustrations in "Daily Graphic," 5th November, 1900.
November 22nd—Colonel Wilde's command extended for two years.
December 10th— Prize Distribution at Headquarters by General Turner, Inspector General of Auxiliary Forces. Illustrations in "Daily Graphic," 12th December, 1900

Out-door Parades at Chingford and Victoria Park.
Range at Pirbright.
The Church Parade ordered for 24th June was cancelled in consequence of the serious illness of the Acting Chaplain, Rev. Professor Shuttleworth.
Fifty-nine Members of the Corps served in the Army during the year.
In the Pageant at the Royal Military Tournament at Islington, a Detachment appeared in the uniform of the period of 1860; the uniforms were made by Mr. W. Clarkson from particulars supplied by Colonel Wilde.
Officers' Mess at Hotel Cecil.

1901.

February 2nd—A Detachment for Funeral of H.M. Queen Victoria.
March 23rd—Sergeants' Mess Annual Dinner at Headquarters.
May 20th—Officers' Mess (Ladies' Dinner), at Hotel Cecil.
May 27th, Whit Monday—Field Firing at Pirbright.
July 13th—Annual Inspection in Victoria Park; present 914.
July 21st—Church Parade at Christ Church, Newgate Street.
August 3rd to 10th—Brigade Camp at Colchester; 27 Officers and 396 Non-Commissioned Officers and Men.
December 8th—Prize Distribution at Headquarters by Sir Alfred Newton, Bart.
December 13th—Tablet to memory of Private Walker, City Imperial Volunteers, unveiled in St. Lawrence Jewry, Gresham Street. (At request of family there was no ceremony.)

Out-door Parades at Chingford and Victoria Park.
Range at Pirbright.
Forty-eight Members of the Corps served in the Army during the year.
Officers' Mess was held at the Hotel Cecil.

Brigade Bearer Company was made a separate command.

In December, the Hon. Claude G. Hay, M.P., offered a Challenge Cup as a Recruiting Prize.

1902.

March 1st—Military Funeral of Lieutenant N. Duncan-Teape.
May 12th—Officers' Mess (Ladies' Dinner), at Hotel Cecil.
May 19th, Whit Monday—Field Firing at Pirbright.
June 14th—Authority given to receive the four Maxim Machine Guns of City Imperial Volunteers.
June 29th—Detachment at Shoreditch Parish Church on occasion of attendance of Mayor and Corporation.
July 5th—Headquarters used for King's Dinner.
July 5th—Annual Inspection in Hyde Park; present 779.
July 13th—Church Parade, Christ Church, Newgate Street.
August 2nd to 9th—Brigade Camp at Yarmouth; 28 Officers, 471 Non-Commissioned Officers and Men.
August 9th—Detachment for Coronation of T.M. King Edward VII. and Queen Alexandra.
October 25th—Detachments for Royal Progress of T.M. King Edward VII. and Queen Alexandra.
December 8th—Prize Distribution at Headquarters by Colonel Vesey Dawson, C.V.O.

Out-door Parades at Chingford and in Victoria Park.

Ranges at Pirbright and Ilford.

The Battalion was attached to the 2nd London Volunteer Infantry Brigade under the Irish Guards.

In Brigade Orders of 7th May a Brigade Transport Company was formed.

Fifteen Members of the Corps served in the Army during the year.

1903.

January 24th—Retirement of Colonel Wilde gazetted.
January 31st—Captain and Honorary Major A. H. Locke to be Major.
February—Silver belts for Officers abolished, and new pattern waist-belts ordered to be worn.
February 3rd—Death of Lieutenant G. E. Colebrook. Extract from Battalion Orders:—" The Commanding Officer announces with extreme regret the death on the 3rd inst. (the result of a motor car accident), of Lieutenant G. E. Colebrook, a most promising Officer and one who took the greatest interest in his duties."
February 4th—Lieutenant-Colonel Vickers Dunfee to command.

February 4th—Major E. V. Wellby to be Lieutenant-Colonel.
March—Appointment of Assistant Drill Instructors abolished.
April 15th—Captain and Quarter-Master Charles Davis resigns. Extract from Battalion Orders:—" By the resignation of Captain and Quarter-Master C. Davis, the Battalion loses the seivices of an Officer who has devoted much time and attention to his duties and always gave the interests of the Battalion his constant care."
April 18th—Regimental Handbook for 1903 published. .
May 8th—Designation altered to Fourth Volunteer Battalion of The Royal Fusiliers (City of London Regiment).

PERSONAL REMINISCENCES OF THE AUTHOR.

IT has been suggested to me that I might close this book with my personal recollections of some of the events recorded therein.

It was in 1861, when I was about to join the ranks of the Victoria Rifles, who then had pleasant headquarters in Marlborough Place, St. John's Wood, that I was offered a Commission in the 6th Tower Hamlets Rifle Volunteer Corps, and on 5th June, 1861, was gazetted Ensign, receiving in due course my Commission from the Lord Lieutenant of the Tower, Viscount Combermere, who also signed my Commission on promotion to Lieutenant, 21st November, 1862. Certain fees had to be paid to the Clerk.

Uniform was the first thing to see to, and I obtained the full dress—a red-grey tunic, with full and long skirts, trimmed with much silver lace on the sleeves, a low shako with waving white feather plumes (the men wore white horse-hair), red Morocco belts, the cross belt having a large badge in the centre, with chain and whistle; trousers were of the same material as the tunic, with a red and white cord; also undress, a black frock similar to the Guards; black trousers, with an oak-leaf braid stripe; black waistbelt, and stiff cap with peak. Among all the many changes in my uniform this pattern cap alone continued to be worn until the field service cap came in recently.

In these early days there were no grants, so a kind of purchase system was in vogue, Officers making donations on joining, and on promotion, according to rank.

My first parade in uniform was on Sunday, 9th June, 1861, when I carried to Church one of the pair of silk Colours, which had been presented to the Corps.

On 3rd July, I was with the Guard of Honour at the Ironmongers' Almshouses in Hackney Road, for Presentation of Colours to the 4th Corps.

There were then no facilities to learn drill; but after some trouble I was attached to the Scots Fusilier Guards, quartered at the barracks in Ordnance Road, St. John's Wood, and duly attended there at 6 o'clock every morning to master the intricate drill then in vogue, with its fixed No. 1 Company and rigid front. The first drill book I had was "Field Exercise, 1859," since which I have studied at least thirteen different drill books, down to "Infantry Drill, 1902."

The "Battalion" consisted of defaulters, and varied greatly in strength each day; it presented a somewhat mixed appearance, as the men were in various kit—from full dress to fatigue—according to the nature of their offences. After drill I used to work out the problems with a box of matches.

Sergeant-Instructor M'Blain I remember very well, he was afterwards Sergeant-Major, and was appointed Quarter-Master of the Scots Guards, in 1869.

On the termination of my attendance I received from the Adjutant the following Certificate, which is probably the first given to an Officer of Volunteers.

[*Copy*.]   PORTMAN STREET BARRACKS, LONDON.
30*th September*, 1861.

I certify that Ensign Wilde of the 6th Tower Hamlets Volunteers has been attached to the 1st Battalion Scots Fusilier Guards from the 24th June to the 31st July, 1861, for Instruction in Drills, and that he understands Company Drill and can also take charge of a Company in Battalion Drill. He has also a knowledge of Light Infantry.

(Signed) W. R. TREFUSIS,
Adjutant,
1st B.S.F.G.

To ENSIGN WILDE,
6th Tower Hamlets Volunteers.

I was drilling in the Tower Moat on 22nd June, 1861, when the great fire in Tooley Street broke out. The parade had to be dismissed in consequence of the large burning particles blown across the river. The conflagration was a very magnificent sight viewed from the Tower ; the river was ablaze with floating burning oil.

On 11th September, 1861, I was in command of the Cadets of the Corps at the Review at the Crystal Palace.

Drills were then on Tuesdays or Thursdays, in plain clothes, with parades in uniform nearly every Saturday at some School or other large room, as it was not till August, 1861, that the premises at 112, Shaftesbury Street were taken for Headquarters. The hall was an old theatre, looking very ruinous when first inspected ; the seats were broken and rotting ; the stage was encumbered with torn and damaged scenery. The ground, which was then on a level with the floor of the hall, had been a tea-garden, and the remains of arbours were round it. The place had been shut up for some time, having been taken by the owners of a neighbouring Theatre to prevent opposition performances.

Putting the place in proper order and repair and filling up the ground to its present level was a very costly job, and involved the Regiment in litigation for many years. The first Parade in the drill ground was on Saturday, 25th April, 1862.

One of the great events of the year was the Easter Monday Review, for which we mustered about 4 a.m. in the City to proceed to Brighton or elsewhere, when a great deal of powder was burnt, to the satisfaction of the crowds who assembled on the occasion ; the operations always ended with a March Past before the General Commanding. It was not for many years that the Officers took quarters for the Easter Week, the railway allowing us to go down earlier and return later in uniform, and many were the discussions as to what was sufficient uniform to pass with the tickets.

In 1862 I was at my first Easter Monday Field Day, parading in the City at 6 a.m. for Brighton; we had about three hours' fall-out after the march past, getting back to London Bridge after midnight.

Whit Monday was another Field Day date, when journeys were made to some Nobleman's country park for operations, often, I am afraid, of rather a picnic character, and we have had Parades on Good Fridays and Boxing Days.

Inspections were generally carefully rehearsed, a programme of the manœuvres to be done being issued.

There were often Marches out, with a visit to the parks for blank firing which indeed was sometimes performed in the drill ground.

The Sixth was in all the Metropolitan gatherings, and I managed to be always out with the Battalion.

Several changes in parts of the uniform were made, the plumes were given up for tufts, the shakos were made higher, belts were changed to black; the Officers had no Mess uniform until the early seventies, when a black jacket with rolled collar and red waistcoat was adopted, as we could not face a jacket of the grey cloth.

On 9th June, 1862, I went to Earl Cowper's, Panshanger, for a Field Day. We were conveyed by the Great Northern Railway, in cattle trucks, in which boards had been fixed across for seats. It was rough travelling. Coming back we were turned out at Holloway instead of being conveyed to King's Cross.

On 18th October, we left Shoreditch for Harwich at half-past twelve noon, arriving there about 4 o'clock. It was pouring with rain, so that the operations, in which Regulars from Colchester were to have taken part, had to be abandoned, and we got back to town about midnight.

I was present with the Corps on 7th March, 1863, and marched to and from Headquarters, when 18,000 Metropolitan Volunteers were in Hyde Park on the occasion of the Princess

Alexandra of Denmark making her entry into London. Was at the Queen's Birthday Review in Hyde Park on 28th May, 1864, when 22,000 Volunteers were present; we mustered in Finsbury Square at 2.30, marching thence to the Park. On 20th April, 1865, I was presented at the Levee.

In January, 1866, I was promoted Captain, receiving a new Commission from Sir John Burgoyne, who was at the time Lord Lieutenant of the Tower. On 23rd June, there was a Review in Hyde Park, when about 12,000 Volunteers marched past the Duke of Cambridge.

In July, 1867, the Belgian Volunteers came over; they received medals from the Prince of Wales at Wimbledon on 13th July—a pouring wet day. I also attended the great Ball given at the Agricultural Hall on 18th. On Saturday, 20th, there was a Review and March Past at Wimbledon before the Sultan; another very wet day.

I took my turn of duty at Headquarters during the Fenian alarm, and was sworn in as a Special Constable for Marylebone on 23rd December, 1867, and afterwards was busy drilling at Lords.

Easter, 1868, Review was at Portsmouth, where we took a house on the Parade; on Monday, 13th April, the operations were assisted by war ships and gun boats and some regular troops. On 20th June we had a muster of 431 at the Review by the Queen at Windsor.

In 1869, Easter Monday fell on 29th March. A Field Day was fixed to be held at Dover, where the Officers had taken quarters on Marine Parade; the weather in the morning was so exceedingly bad that orders were issued to cancel the Review, but the Duke of Cambridge arriving later, when the weather had improved, caused the troops to be mustered and the operations to be carried out as arranged.

On November 25th, 1869, I attended at Buckingham Palace with the National Testimonial Deputation to present an Address to the King of the Belgians from the Volunteers.

I attended the first School of Instruction held at Wellington Barracks in October, 1870, obtaining a Captain's Certificate, which was all written out. I obtained leave to attend again on the 15th of the next month and received a Certificate of Proficiency as Field Officer, in War Office Form 544, dated 30th November, 1870. Both my Certificates were signed by Colonel Richard Monck, Commanding School of Instruction. Drill was 10 to 1 and 3.30 to 5 p.m. daily.

I do not know of anything very special to record of our doings at this time. There were the usual parades at Headquarters on Saturdays, in uniform, with a March to the Tower, Victoria Park, Hackney Downs, Charterhouse, or some other open space for drill, and perhaps blank firing.

Volunteering was altering very much, efficiency conditions had to be complied with, and a feeling of the importance of the duties undertaken was growing.

I performed the duties of Acting Adjutant on several occasions.

In 1872, the Easter Monday Review was at Brighton on 1st April; the Officers were invited to a Grand Ball at the Pavilion, given to Prince Arthur.

In May, two Sergeants of the Guards were engaged to give instruction in the then new drill at Headquarters.

In September, the English Volunteers were invited to the Belgian fêtes; we were received by the King, and magnificently entertained both publicly and privately—Banquets, Balls, Special Performances at the Theatre at Ghent and Brussels. Several Officers of the Corps went with me, and we thoroughly enjoyed ourselves.

A Reception was held at the Mansion House, 4th March, 1873, for presentation by the Lady Mayoress of the Anglo-Belgian prizes won at the fêtes last September.

Negotiations and communications passed for the amalgamation of the Sixth Corps with the already united Second and Fourth. Matters were finally settled to the satisfaction of all concerned, and on 1st January, 1874, the Tower Hamlets Rifle Volunteer Brigade was completed. There was a great deal of work to do in carrying out the necessary arrangements and making a new roll of the 1006 Members of the three Corps; my number was 68.

The grey uniform of the three Corps was very similar except that the Sixth did not wear a red stripe on their trousers, so I had to have this alteration made. A change of uniform was soon taken in hand, but it was not till November, 1874, that authority was received to adopt scarlet, with blue facings, retaining the shako; the change was made very gradually. I appeared in scarlet for the first time at the Prize Distribution, 22nd December, 1875.

In 1876 I arranged for a Detachment to march to Tring, where there was to be a Field Day on Easter Monday, 17th April. The Detachment under my command, of 5 Officers and 40 Men with 23 Drums and Fifes, started from Headquarters on Saturday, 15th, for Watford (Clarendon Hotel). On Sunday, after Church Parade, we marched to Berkhampstead, and on Monday morning to Tring, joining the Battalion for the Field Day, and returning with it to town in the evening. Each man paid his own expenses. The weather was fine, but cold, with a good deal of snow about. The scheme was successfully carried out. I had been over the ground previously, and made all arrangements for quarters in lofts and barns.

July 1st there was a Review in Hyde Park by the Prince of Wales, of Regulars, Militia and Volunteers; we mustered at Finsbury Square, marching to Grosvenor Square to join our Brigade; after the Review we kept the ground for the Inspection of the Queen's Westminsters, they doing the same for us. It was a long day's work.

On the 17th March, 1877, was the celebrated Route March of Lord Abinger, of the Guards and his Volunteer Brigade. We started from the Mansion House, along the Embankment, Pall Mall, St. James' Street, Piccadilly, etc.

The Marching Column last Easter was such a success that I organised another, to proceed viâ Watford, on Saturday, 31st March; St. Albans, Sunday, 1st April; thence by rail on Easter Monday to Dunstable, to join the Battalion for the Field Day, and returning with them. We were 5 Officers and about 60 Non-Commissioned Officers and Men. Each man paid his own expenses. The weather was favourable, and all the arrangements worked out satisfactorily.

On 9th June, Lord Abinger marched the Guards with the Scots Guards Volunteer Brigade (which we then belonged to) from Wellington Barracks to Wimbledon for a Field Day; it was a hot day and many men fell out, the hill from Wandsworth to the Common telling heavily.

Again in 1878 I arranged for another Marching Column at Easter, although there were no operations on Easter Monday. I started on Saturday, 20th April, with 6 Officers, 64 Non-Commissioned Officers and Men, and 19 Drums, Fifes and 3 Buglers, for Watford, where the 2nd Herts. came out to meet us. After Church Parade on Sunday, we marched on to St. Albans, the local Brass Band playing us in, and thence marching back to Headquarters on Monday. Guards were always mounted at the Headquarters at night.

On 27th July, 1878, I attended my first Camp at Aldershot, being in command of a Company to join the 3rd Provisional Battalion. We had a fine weather week. Previously to going to Camp, the Detachment practised tent pitching on Hackney Downs.

I was gazetted Major, 20th May, 1879, and in due course received this time a Queen's Commission as Major, "or such higher rank as I may be appointed to"; it is signed by the Duke of Cambridge as Commander in Chief, and Mr. Childers as Secretary of State for War.

I went as Captain in Command of the Company to Camp with a Provisional Battalion at Aldershot, on 5th July.

In March, 1880, I went through a Course of Equitation at the Regent's Park Barracks, obtaining a Certificate in usual form.

There was an Easter Monday Field Day at Brighton this year; the Officers had quarters for the week in the King's Road.

I could not go to Camp as there was no vacancy in the Provisional Battalion for a Major.

We were busy on changes in uniform; helmets had taken the place of the shako, a patrol jacket was adopted for Officers undress, and swords were altered.

In 1881, I was at Brighton for Easter Monday Field Day on 18th April, in same quarters as last year.

On 9th July, I was at the large Review of Volunteers by the Queen at Windsor. Paraded at Finsbury, 8.30 a.m. train from Broad Street to Datchet, crossing river on a pontoon bridge; back in London, 11 p.m.

On 6th August, I took a Detachment to a Provisional Battalion at Aldershot.

Easter Monday, 10th April, 1882, the operations were at Portsmouth, the Officers as usual taking quarters from the previous Thursday. General Moncrieff was in command of our Brigade. It was a very fine day.

On 6th June, I passed in tactics; it was the first examination held.

The Field Day was at Brighton on Easter Monday, 1883, 26th March. March Past was first. The Officers had quarters in King's Road. Snow and very cold.

I was Senior Major of the Provisional Battalion at Aldershot, 11th to 18th August, taking down a strong Detachment.

The Easter operations in 1884 were at Dover, where the Officers had quarters from 10th to 15th April; it was a fine day. The day finished with a March Past.

Easter Monday, 1885, 2nd April, I was with the Battalion at Brighton, the Officers establishing their Mess at Markwells' Royal Hotel. March Past on Race Course before Field Day.

April 9th, 1886, I was gazetted Hon. Lieutenant-Colonel.

I was with the Marching Column, under command of General Moncrieff, at Easter. Train was taken on Good Friday, 23rd April, part of the way, when we had some outpost work about Bridge. I was quartered by myself in a farm house, but the General was kind enough to get me an invitation to the Hall where he was staying. On Saturday we had a great fight near Lydden, troops from Dover coming out to oppose us; however we finally were able to join the Mess established in Waterloo Crescent.

In August I had a strong Detachment at Aldershot with the 5th Provisional Battalion. There was the usual Field Day. We had one night of outpost—cold work it was, I remember.

In 1887, I was in command of the 9th Provisional Battalion, composed of 1st and 2nd Tower Hamlets and our Gardners, of the Easter Marching Column. On Good Friday, 8th April, we took train to Canterbury for a fight near that place; later, there was a night attack. On the Saturday, we had a long heavy march to Dover; on Easter Monday, the Field Day.

On 14th May, the Queen opened the People's Palace, and we were on duty in the Whitechapel Road.

The 2nd of July, the Metropolitan Volunteers marched past the Queen at Buckingham Palace, the troops were moved along the Mall to the Palace and away to the Embankment.

The following Saturday, the 9th, was a Grand March Past before the Queen at Aldershot. As Colonel Wigram had a Brigade, I was in command of the Battalion. We left Waterloo at 5 a.m.; had breakfast on the field. After the March Past the troops were formed in two lines of Quarter Columns facing inwards, the Queen driving through on her way from the saluting base. We got back to our rendezvous at 3.30 quite ready for another meal. The dust was awful, everyone was black with it. We reached Waterloo again at 10.30 p.m.

Good Friday, 30th March, 1888, I was in command of a Battalion of the Marching Column under Lord Methuen; we trained to Ashford, where operations commenced. At the end of the day most of the Officers were driven to quarters in Folkestone, coming out the next morning to the positions for the day's manœuvres, which ended at Dover; it was very cold, with a good deal of snow on the road sides. On Easter Monday, I commanded the Battalion in the day's operation between Folkestone and Dover.

On 11th August, I went to Aldershot, joining the Second Provisional Battalion for a week, with 150 men and the Gardners; we had very fine weather. On the Thursday, we had a heavy day, being under arms for over twelve hours. On 15th December, I was gazetted Lieutenant-Colonel and Honorary Colonel.

Camp in 1889 was for six days' only, going down on Saturday, 3rd, and returning Thursday, 8th. With the 3rd London, we formed a Provisional Battalion. There was a Field Day and March Past for the German Emperor on Romping Downs, on Wednesday, 7th, some 150 men coming down to join the Battalion for the day. A large number of troops were out.

In 1890 nothing beyond usual parades occurred. On 23rd November I succeeded to Command.

The events of my Command are recorded in previous pages.

I have Commanded the Battalion when it has taken part in any operations, except on those occasions when I have been appointed to a Brigade.

On several occasions I took part in "War Games" as commanding a force or otherwise, and as an Assistant Umpire.

December 19th, 1892, I attended at the Levee Room, Horse Guards, at the first distribution of the Volunteer Officers' Decoration by the Duke of Cambridge. I wore it at the Prize Distribution at Headquarters the same evening, so was probably the first Officer wearing the Decoration at a public function.

In November, 1900, my term of command was extended for two years.

On 23rd January, 1903, I was gazetted out, with permission to retain my rank and wear the uniform on my retirement.

During my twelve years of command, I have the satisfaction to know that the Regiment continued to go forward, a result greatly due to the good feeling of all ranks, and the hearty assistance and co-operation at all times accorded me.

E. T. Rodney Wilde
Col.

INDEX.

	PAGE
Active Service	55
Adjutants, Former	78
Amalgamation of Sixth Corps	24
Ambulance	38
Anderson, Quarter-Master	28
Annual Inspection	19, 42
Annual Returns	57, 68, 69, 70
Auxiliaries of Trained Bands	3, 4
Badge	9, 27
Barnett, E. de B.	29
Battalion Challenge Cup	47
Bethune, D. E. B. Patton	30
Bignell, Colour-Sergeant	35
Brigade Bearer Company	39, 41
Brigade Camps	34, 35, 40, 42
Bugle, Silver	52
Burge, B. H.	17, 26
Cadet Corps	19
Camps	13, 34, 35, 46
Challenge Cups	18, 40, 42, 47, 49, 50, 51
Challenge Shields	48, 51
Change of Designation	60
Chaplain	15, 36
Church Parade	19, 36
City Imperial Volunteers	43, 55
Clapton Cup, First	50
Clapton Cup, Second	50
Coddington, H. A.	30
Colours	3, 9, 15, 18
Coningham, Henry	32
Cups	18, 40
Cyclists	45
Death	16, 28, 29, 30, 31, 32, 33, 35, 36, 41
Designation	28, 60

	PAGE
Distribution of Prizes	24, 34
Drill Competition	21
Duncan-Teape, N.	35
Drum, Old	11
Dunfee, Vickers	32, 33, 41, 42
East London Volunteer Infantry Brigade	28, 39
Easter	15, 23, 29, 34, 41, 42
Events, Record of	79
Fenian Alarm	19
Field Days	22, 34
Field Firing	46
Field Service Cap	28
First Clapton Cup	51
First Tower Hamlets Volunteer Rifle Corps	25
Flag of 1643	3
Fletcher, Banister	24, 32, 38
Former Adjutants	78
Former Officers	71
Former Sergeant-Majors	78
Fourth Tower Hamlets Corps	15
Funerals	28, 35, 37
Fusion of 2nd and 4th Corps	14
Gardner Machine Guns	41
Guards of Honour	15, 24, 34, 35
Honourable Artillery Company	4, 18, 55
Hay, Claude (Hon.) M.P.	44, 51
Hay, Claude, Challenge Cup	51
Headquarters	13, 17, 18, 37, 38
Holmes' Challenge Cup	47
Holt, John	13, 26, 28, 29
House of Commons Return	5, 6
Ladies' Challenge Cup	40
Localization	28
Long Service Medal	54
Lowry, Armar	13, 14, 26, 29
Machine Guns	41
Mapleson, J. H.	17, 26, 29, 31
Marching Columns	29, 41, 42
Maude, R. J.	29
Maxim Machine Guns	43, 44, 55
Medals	21, 24, 35, 57

	PAGE
Memorial Tablets	57
Moncrieff, G. H.	30, 31, 41
Money, C. G. C.	30
Money, G. H.	17
Morris Tube Range	46
Muster Roll, Ratcliff Volunteers	10
Muster, Trained Bands	3, 4
National Rifle Association Meeting	23, 24, 34, 46
Newton, Sir Alfred J., Bart.	43, 44, 55
Nominal Roll	53, 56
North East London Rifles	17, 18, 25
Officers' Decoration	53
Officers Serving	61
Officers Retired	71
Officers' Mess	36
Original Tower Hamlets Corps	12
Pay and Allowances (1803)	7
Personal Reminiscences of the Author	96
Philharmonic Cup	18, 49
Print, Ratcliff Volunteer	11
Prize Distributions	24, 34
Prize (General Moncrieff's)	31
Prize (Hon. Claude Hay, M.P.)	51
Provisional Battalions	34
Quarter-Master's Cup	51
Ranges	19, 34
Ratcliff Volunteers	10, 11
Record of Events	79
Regimental Challenge Cup	18, 47, 50
Relics	9, 10, 11
Retired Officers	71
Returns (Annual)	68
Returns (House of Commons)	5, 6
Reviews	3, 4, 5, 13, 15, 22, 23, 34, 35
Richardson, E. R. S.	29
Roll (Nominal)	53, 56
Route March	34
Royal East India Volunteers	11
Schreiber, F. B.	14, 15, 29
Second Clapton Cup	51
Second Tower Hamlets Corps	13

	PAGE
Second London Volunteer Infantry Brigade	28, 41
Sergeant Majors	15, 17, 37, 78
Sergeants' Mess	36, 37
Sergeants Serving	65
Shields	48, 51
Shooting	46
Shuttleworth, H. C.	36
Signalling	45
Sixth Tower Hamlets Corps	17, 25
South Africa, Service in	57
Strength of Tower Hamlets Regiment, 1643	3
Subscriptions	15, 17, 18
Teape, N. Duncan	35
Thomson, James	16, 48
Thomson Shield	48
Tower Hamlets Corps (1860)	12
Tower Hamlets Regiment (1800)	3, 4, 5, 6
Tower Hamlets Rifle Volunteer Brigade	12, 14, 15, 24, 25, 60
Trained Bands	3, 4
Uniforms	7, 13, 15, 17, 19, 27, 28, 42
Volunteer Long Service Medal	54
Volunteer Officers' Decoration	53
Walker, Colonel	13
Walmisley, C. N.	17
War Games	36
Wellby, E. V.	32, 33, 43, 51, 55, 57
White, O. M.	40, 41
Whit Monday	15, 22
Wigram, Clifford	13, 26, 28, 31, 33
Wilde, E. T. R.	19, 24, 26, 29, 31, 32, 33, 35, 53
Wimbledon	23, 24, 34

PRINTED BY
CONINGHAM BROS.,
797, COMMERCIAL ROAD, LONDON, E.

Ingram Content Group UK Ltd.
Milton Keynes UK
UKHW021821170323
418736UK00007B/416